ESTRENO Collection of Contemporary Spanish Plays

General Editor: Martha T. Halsey

THE MUSIC WINDOW

ANTONIO BUERO-VALLEJO

THE MUSIC WINDOW

(Música cercana)

Translated by Marion Peter Holt

ESTRENO
University Park, Pennsylvania
1994

ESTRENO Contemporary Spanish Plays 5
General Editor: Martha T. Halsey
Department of Spanish, Italian and Portuguese
College of the Liberal Arts
The Pennsylvania State University
University Park, PA 16802 USA

Library of Congress Cataloging in Publication Data
Buero-Vallejo, Antonio, 1916-
The Music Window
Translation of: Música cercana
Contents: The Music Window
1. Buero-Vallejo, Antonio,1916-   Translation, English
I. Holt, Marion Peter. II. Title.
Library of Congress Catalog Card No.: 93-74274
ISBN: 0-9631212-4-3

This edition has been translated
with financial assistance of the
Spanish Dirección General del Libro y Bibliotecas
of the Ministerio de Cultura
and published with assistance of the
Consulate General of Spain in New York

Cover: Jeffrey Eads

A NOTE ON THE PLAY

The Music Window (*Música cercana*) by Antonio Buero-Vallejo introduces us to Alfredo, an aging financier drawn home to his estranged daughter on a mission of reclamation. Isolated for years on his country estate, Alfredo has put together a video called "Time in my Hands": taking photographs of himself at different ages, he has linked them together using computer technology to create a moving picture of himself over the years. With this tool he can observe his face aging and growing younger over and over again. Alfredo hopes that by fixing the image at key moments in his life he can gain a point of entry for his unreliable memories, perhaps even capturing man's most elusive dream, to change the past. As his daughter's lover observes,

"...he is looking for something perhaps forgotten. Something that torments him more than other things. Maybe he wants to stop time to catch that forgotten enigma of surprise. As if he opened a window on the enigma."

Although Alfredo has come back home to be with his family, he remains a vague and mysterious figure to those around him. The people who inhabit his present-day reality—his venal son, his daughter straining for independence, the embittered family servant known as "Mommy," his daughter's freethinking revolutionist lover—are pushed to the margins of Alfredo's consciousness by his obsessive memories of a strange woman next door whom he has loved from afar since childhood. Alfredo strains to bring the conflicting worlds of past, present and fantasy into balance, using modern technology in an effort to make time stand still. But ultimately his dealings with the modern world destroy all hope of attaining the happiness he so desperately seeks.

Buero-Vallejo's plays take place in the intersection of perception and reality, asking us to question the ultimate nature of human contact. Theatrically, with his use of multiple staging and shifting time-frames, Buero-Vallejo presents a concrete image of Alfredo's dismantled, unstable world. In Marion Peter Holt's precise and poetic translation, *The Music Window* moves inexorably to a shattering resolution, in which Alfredo's intrigues conspire to strip away his self-deception.

Royston Coppenger, Executive Director
National Theater Translation Fund

Antonio Buero-Vallejo

Photo Credit: Candyce Leonard

ABOUT THE PLAYWRIGHT

Antonio Buero-Vallejo (b. 1916) is Spain's best known contemporary dramatist—if we exclude Fernando Arrabal, whose international recognition began with the French versions of his early plays. Buero's multimedia exploration of the effects of political repression on the aged Goya, *The Sleep of Reason*, has been translated into more than a dozen languages and has been staged by such eminent directors as Andrzej Wajda and Liviu Ciulei. *The Foundation* (1974), dealing with a young political prisoner's delusory rejection of reality, and *The Concert at St. Ovide Fair* (1962), focusing on the exploitation of a group of blind musicians by a Parisian impresario in 1771, have been performed throughout Europe, and both plays have had professional stagings in the United States.

Since the production of his Artaudian historical drama *The Detonation* in 1977, Buero has written five plays, produced at intervals of two to three years, which focus on contemporary society and individuals who are compelled to acknowledge the deceptions in their lives or confront an obsession or a traumatizing event of the past. Invariably these plays invite audiences to experience a highly theatrical "realism" which includes the scenic depiction of inner "realities," through inventive uses of sound and music as co-signifiers with dialogue and often startling lighting shifts and effects. Buero's aural and visual devices to bring his audiences into closer identification psychologically or physically with his protagonists have been appropriately called "immersion-effects"—a term coined by the Spanish critic Ricardo Doménech in the early 1970s.

In *The Music Window*, the thematic visual element is the presence of a young girl, seemingly untouched by time, seated in a window listening to recordings of orchestral music. A quite different visual element is the projected video that represents the obsessive attempt of an overbearing and insensitive entrepreneur to place "time in my hands" (as he expresses it) by recreating stages of his life through computerized video editing. Like his two great predecessors, Valle-Inclán and Lorca, Buero has boldly challenged traditional stage realism as well as audience expectations, and his scenic concepts for plays that depend on both word and image in their logical development exploit all the technical possibilities of the modern theatre.

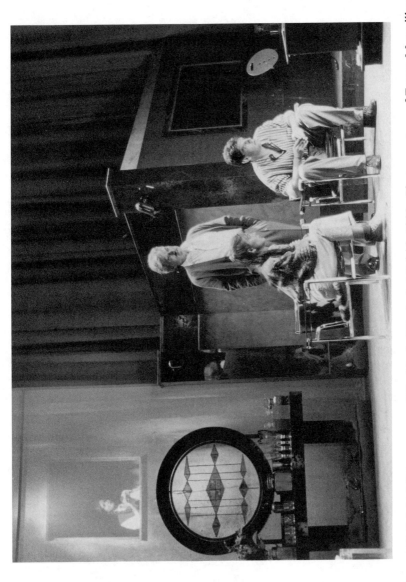

Antonio Buero-Vallejo's *Música cercana* (*The Music Window*), Madrid, 1989. Photo courtesy of Teatro Maravillas (Madrid).

CHARACTERS

Alfredo
Sandra
Lorenza (frequently called "Mommy")
Javier
René
Isolina (who never speaks)

In our time.

PLAYWRIGHT'S NOTE: The characters and the plot of this play are fictitious. Any similarity with real persons and events is coincidental and should not be considered an allusion to them.

TRANSLATOR'S NOTE: In the original Spanish version of the play, the character Lorenza (also referred to as "Mommy") occasionally reveals her disgust and punctuates the moment with a blunt comment or word in English, which is not understood by the character she is addressing. For the English version, the languages have simply been reversed. These phrases, in contrast to the expected speech of the character who utters them, are now in Spanish. English-speaking audiences will react essentially as Spanish audiences reacted to the unexpected English words and phrases. For the director who might prefer to have Lorenza say these lines as asides in English the original words are retained in brackets.

THE SET

Entrances and exits downstage left and right. Grey curtains or flats frame the entire scenic space. A small sitting room or den occupies the greater part of the stage. Only on the sides, and perhaps upstage right, should the walls reach a normal height. The upstage wall slants from the right, dropping to a height of three or four feet from the floor, continuing horizontally toward the left some distance and then rising obliquely to the upper edge of a modern window with metal frame and two panes. The wall then slants down again to its previous height in such a way that the window is inserted in a kind of triangle of wall, cut off at the top and standing out as a special focus of interest. The left wall, perhaps uneven in the same way as its starting point upstage, soon reaches its normal height. Against it is a bookcase. Downstage right, a door, generally open.

A sectional sofa is placed parallel to the right and the upstage wall; in front of it, one or two glass top tables with ashtrays, lighters, cigarette holders, magazines, and a vase for flowers. Between the sofa and the window a small table with telephone and a computer monitor. Under the window, a bar. In the left corner of the room, another computer screen higher up. Far downstage and toward the left, three small easy chairs and a low stand with a portable television set and VCR, with its back to the audience. It is placed low enough for those seated facing it to be easily seen. Valuable paintings and drawings on the walls; somewhere a modern statuette. The whole of the space, in its sobriety, denotes wealth and appears to be part of an older apartment which has been remodeled for comfort.

The downstage left edge of the sitting room meets an almost frontal wall that encompasses a good part of the remaining space up to the far left of the stage and creates a quite different playing area. A short sofa and table with a cradle phone are the bare essentials of the impersonal ambience -- as suitable for the corner of some office as for a modest tea room. Over the sofa and across the wall, a huge graph, complete with labels, numbers and ascending colored lines, indicating the progress of a business enterprise. The graph can be easily slipped aside or raised. When this happens, a window similar in size to the graph is revealed. Behind the window, dense greenery.

Beyond the cutaway upstage wall, the suggestion of an adjacent courtyard; at some distance, upstage center, a wide facing wall. Illuminated at times by the indirect sunlight that reaches it, it stands out like a strange rectangular apparition, for in the naked glare of its flaking surface we can make out only one window with an old roll-up blind or wooden shutters and thick curtains. Situated in the middle of the wall and higher than the window of the sitting room, it is located so that it is completely visible over the wall of the principal room from all viewing points. Adjustments can be made to provide a large screen on which the video seen on the television set by the characters on stage will be projected. This can disappear or remain in shadow when not in use.

This suggested scenic layout accommodates the action of the play, but it could be quite different. In any case, it is essential that the window in the courtyard wall be visible at all times, and perhaps it should appear closer than its normal distance, as if some subjective obsession were drawing it closer. The complete visibility of the projection screen is also essential.

PART ONE

(Before the lights come up, Mozart's Concerto No. 1 in G Major for flute and orchestra grows louder and then its sound begins to fade as a cold, vaguely lunar light rises over the courtyard window. At almost the same time the television set emerges from the darkness. It is turned on and throws its blue-grey brightness on the faces of the three persons who are watching it. SANDRA, an attractive young woman about 25, dressed in casual attire, is slouched on the small easy chair at stage left. In the chair next to her is LORENZA, a well-preserved woman of 65, wearing a dark house dress. SHE watches the video a bit indifferently. Standing behind them, ALFREDO, age 56, with well groomed grey hair, good bearing, and a confident and agreeable appearance. HE is wearing light colored slacks and an elegant woven jacket and has a glass in his hand. As HE notes the effect the video is having on the two women, HE takes a sip from his glass. The video reaches its end and stops. At the same moment the light turns to clear morning; on the courtyard wall, sunlight and a slanting bluish shadow. The music is now very faint.)

ALFREDO: Shall I run it back? To age 20, maybe?

SANDRA *(Fearing he will.)*: No need.

ALFREDO: Then I'll rewind. *(HE uses a remote control which is left on top of the set. HE takes a few steps back and, hiding his amusement, turns around and faces SANDRA.)* What did you think of it?

SANDRA: I don't know.

ALFREDO *(Goes toward the window)*: And what about you, Mommy Lorenza?

LORENZA *(The question seems inappropriate to her.)*: Me? *(ALFREDO leaves his glass on the bar.)*

SANDRA: I don't quite see what you're trying to do with that video.

ALFREDO *(Laughs)*: Amuse myself. *(Brief pause. HE looks through the window.)* Someone's playing a piece I like. Do you hear it?

LORENZA: Just barely. *(The Mozart Adagio ends at that moment.)*

ALFREDO: What do you know... It's stopped. Or has it?

SANDRA: Yes.

ALFREDO: Even with the window closed you can hear something. That stereo must be very close. Don't you hear it sometimes, Mommy?

LORENZA *(Dryly.)*: Yes. Sometimes. *(SHE goes to the window, opens it a little, listens, and closes it again. SANDRA lights a cigarette.)*

ALFREDO: It's going to be hot before long... I'm glad the apartment's cool. *(Laughs.)* I probably won't go away for the summer.

SANDRA *(Disagreeably surprised.)*: You're going to stay here?

ALFREDO: Why not?

SANDRA: You'd be a lot more comfortable in the country house.

ALFREDO: But without my workplace. And after having everything installed here, I'm not about to have it all carried back to the country.

LORENZA: If you hadn't brought it...

ALFREDO: Now that there's more help here, you don't have to do the cleaning. And you're not going to tell me it's in your way.

LORENZA (*With a sarcastic smile.*): Not in my way.

ALFREDO: Then?

LORENZA: But it is in your daughter's way.

ALFREDO: Are you crazy?

LORENZA: Me? You're the crazy one. Completely loco [crazy]. Excuse me. (*SHE starts to leave.*)

ALFREDO: Speaking in tongues again? (*SHE stops and resumes her exit.*) Wait! (*LORENZA stops again. ALFREDO approaches her.*) Why would my odds and ends be in Sandra's way? (*To SANDRA.*)They aren't, are they?

SANDRA: Your things? No.

ALFREDO (*Smiling, to LORENZA.*): Did you hear that?

LORENZA (*Smiling*): Don't play dumb with me, because you aren't.

ALFREDO (*Containing his amusement*): What do you think, Sandra? Am I dumb? Crazy? Mommy Lorenza is good at insults these days. (*To LORENZA.*) You used to show me more respect.

LORENZA: You used to be in the country or off on one of your trips, and we managed quite nicely here.

SANDRA: Will you both shut up? (*Nervous, SHE gets up and looks at her watch again. Short silence.*)

ALFREDO: I won't say another word. (*While HE picks up his glass to refill it.*) Isn't there something you have to do elsewhere, Mommy?

LORENZA: I'm not quite ready to leave.

SANDRA (*Harshly*): Mommy!

ALFREDO (*Laughing again*): There's nothing you can do with her.

LORENZA: Why have you come to live with us? (*SANDRA, who has been walking around, stops and looks at her father.*)

ALFREDO (*Serious*): You're forgetting that this apartment belongs to me...

LORENZA: You turned it over to your daughter more than two years ago. But you don't have to tell us why you've come. There's no need. (*ALFREDO looks at her fixedly and takes a drink. SANDRA sits on the sofa and observes him.*)

ALFREDO: My dear Sandra, for two years I've hardly ever seen you. Your brother is running our business without a hitch. Why not try a more relaxed life... with you at my side again?

LORENZA: In your old home.

ALFREDO (*Referring to SANDRA.*): If she hadn't come here, I wouldn't have moved back either.

LORENZA: And with you, more servants, and callers, and your goons. And the whole place is turned upside down.

ALFREDO (*Affably*): Don't scold me, Mommy.

SANDRA: You have to understand, Papa. You can't escape from your way of life any longer. But I can.

ALFREDO: Sandra, I needed you. If you had taken a business degree... (*SHE interrupts him with a strident laugh, gets up and crosses.*) Don't laugh. In the final analysis, it's my business that supports you.

SANDRA (*Going close to him*): There are other things that support me and interest me.

ALFREDO: I can imagine what interests you. And I do understand! That video over there isn't so far from what interests you.

SANDRA: That video?

ALFREDO: Yes.

SANDRA (*Contemptuously*): Mechanical recreation.

LORENZA: Don't talk in riddles, dear, just to be different. (*SHE is about to leave and stops when she hears ALFREDO.*)

ALFREDO: I agree! You are being difficult, and not so clever either. But I'll bet it does interest you. Huh?

SANDRA (*As she slowly walks toward him*): I don't know if it interests me or not. I know I don't like it.

LORENZA: It's a horror.

ALFREDO: It's... like a document. Unfinished, of course. Until today, nothing more.

SANDRA: A useless document... (*LORENZA nods several times in agreement.*)

ALFREDO (*Smiles*): Well, I was intending to make another one like it with you.

SANDRA (*Angry*): What?

ALFREDO: I have better material on you... more photographs.

SANDRA: Don't even think about it! (*SHE turns her back to him and, giving a light blow with her fist to the TV set, she sits in one of the easy chairs. Just before, the lights come up on the left playing area and JAVIER enters and begins to dial a number on the phone. HE is about 30, with a determined air about him. HE is wearing a proper light colored business suit. The telephone in the sitting room begins to ring. LORENZA starts to leave.*) Don't go, Mommy Lorenza. (*ALFREDO picks up.*)

LORENZA (*Softly*): In case your friend RENÉ comes...

SANDRA: They'll let him in. (*With a sigh LORENZA crosses her hands and waits.*)

ALFREDO: Hello.

JAVIER: Papa.

ALFREDO (*To SANDRA*): Your brother. Hello, son. Yes?

JAVIER: There are some important matters...

ALFREDO: Which ones?

JAVIER: They need to be discussed.

ALFREDO: Is there any hurry?

JAVIER: Of course! You have to come to the board meeting tomorrow at the bank.

ALFREDO: You go in my place.

JAVIER: Not without talking to you first. Will you come?

ALFREDO: Why don't you take care of it. You have power of attorney.

JAVIER: So you don't want to come. Then I'm coming right over to see you.

ALFREDO: But listen...

JAVIER: Goodbye! (*HE hangs up and exits left. The corner darkens again.*)

ALFREDO (*Hangs up and smiles*): He never wants to deal with anything without consulting me.

SANDRA: Is he coming here?

ALFREDO: So it seems. What time does that teacher of yours arrive?

SANDRA (*Looks at her watch*): Soon. His plane must have landed an hour and a half ago.

ALFREDO: Then I'll go change. (*Starts his exit and stops. Sarcastically*) I wonder why you need a private tutor in literature with all you know about that subject.

SANDRA: Papa, René is wonderful! You'll meet him in a little while. He's going to astound you.

ALFREDO: How long has he been coming here?

SANDRA: A year, more or less.

ALFREDO: A bit longer, I believe.

SANDRA (*Changed*): Yes... it may be. (*ALFREDO starts to leave.*) Aren't you going to take your cassette?

ALFREDO: Leave it here for the time being. (*When HE passes by LORENZA, HE gives her an affectionate kiss on the cheek.*) See you in a little while, old girl. (*HE exits right. SANDRA gets up quickly and starts to tug at the television set.*)

SANDRA: Help me! It's in the way. (*LORENZA pushes on the other side.*)

LORENZA: This knickknack or your father?

SANDRA (*Stops and laughs*): Both! You can see that they're one and the same. (*THEY push it left, with the back of the TV toward the audience.*)

LORENZA: He's crazy.

SANDRA: That's the only thing Javier and I agree on. Crazy.

LORENZA: But not stark raving mad. If I know him, he's crazy like a fox.

SANDRA: What the hell made him come here as if he's returning to a monastery? And the way he's taken over this room, as if there weren't plenty of others! (*LORENZA agrees with a grunt.*) It's the very one René and I like to work in. What a mess!

LORENZA: It was his room when he was a boy.

SANDRA: But it's totally different now!

LORENZA (*Starts to leave*): Well, dear, if you don't need me...

SANDRA: Listen, Mommy. Do you think my father suspects?

LORENZA: (*Stopping*): Have no doubt about that. Even before he came here he was having you watched. (*SANDRA moves around impatiently.*)

SANDRA: And now even more! (*Stops*) Mommy Lorenza, there's something you don't know. He agreed to let me leave the country place and come here to live in my own way. Well, I'm sorry, but he's not going to stop me now. I've bought myself another apartment.

LORENZA: Another apartment?

SANDRA: I have my own money and I'm going to keep my freedom! My father is going to learn once and for all that my life isn't his. Just let him try and stop me now! I haven't told him anything yet, but as soon as I get the new place fixed up, I'm leaving. It will be mine and not his! (*SHE hugs and kisses LORENZA effusively.*) And you're coming with me, Mommy!

LORENZA: Don't fool yourself. Do you think he doesn't know anything about your little transaction?

SANDRA: I did it with absolute secrecy.

LORENZA: Ha! As if he didn't have enough people on his payroll. Don't be foolish, child. You can't take a step without them following you.

SANDRA (*Smiles*): I know very well how to give them the slip. (*SHE steps away and lights another cigarette.*)

LORENZA: Well, I'll bet your father already knows the street and the number.

SANDRA (*Turns around*): Even if he does, he'll have to get used to my independence! I'm an adult now and he has no right to surround me with spies.

LORENZA: If they're protecting you, maybe it isn't so bad...

SANDRA (*Smiling, SHE goes closer.*): Mommy, he's not going to have his way. It'll all turn out fine.

LORENZA (*Without conviction*): Let's hope.

SANDRA: (*SHE hugs and kisses her again.*): You'll see.

LORENZA: Does René know about the new apartment?

SANDRA: Not yet, I'll tell him today. (*RENÉ has appeared in the doorway without their noticing. HE is approaching 30; HE is wearing jeans and a tasteful leather jacket, and HE is carrying a leather briefcase. His speech is faintly different from that of the other characters.*)

RENÉ: What is it you're going to tell me today?

SANDRA: René! (*SHE runs and throws herself in his arms as he tosses his briefcase on the sofa. SHE kisses him repeatedly, and HE her; LORENZA turns her back on them with a half-smile. THEY separate, still holding hands.*)

RENÉ: (*Turns his head a little without taking his eyes off SANDRA*): Hello, Ma'am.

LORENZA: Good morning, young man. It's a good thing you've come back.

RENÉ: And tell me why it's a good thing.

LORENZA: Because she was becoming unbearable.

SANDRA: (*Embarrassed*): That's not true!

LORENZA: Sure. It's not true. Can I fix you something?

RENÉ (*To SANDRA*): I tried to get in with my key, but the lock's been changed. And just who is that fellow who let me in and wanted to know my name?

SANDRA: I'll explain. We have more staff now. (*SHE leads him by the hand to the two easy chairs where THEY sit down.*) I thought these two months would never end, René. Didn't they seem awfully long to you too? (*Absolutely delighted, LORENZA crosses to the bar.*)

RENÉ (*Smiles*): We did talk on the phone a lot...

SANDRA: But we couldn't see each other.

LORENZA (*In a low voice, afraid of disturbing them*): Can I fix you something? (*THEY ignore her.*)

SANDRA: Did it all go well?

RENÉ: Very well. Two committees working to help my country, each with its newsletter. And the contributions are up. There are some marvelous people working there. I had to take a side trip to Paris...

SANDRA: You didn't tell me that.

RENÉ: It was only for two days. I went to solicit a grant from the European Committee to pay the rent for one of the offices... They're very poor in that area.

SANDRA: René, you know that I can...

RENÉ: No, Sandra. You've already given us too much. So! Let's get back to talking about books! (*HE gets up.*) I've brought you a sensational video on Rabelais. Do you want to see it? (*HE goes to the VCR and is about to remove the cassette that is in it.*) I have it in my briefcase.

SANDRA: Wait! Don't take that one out yet. My father said to leave it there

RENÉ: Your father?

LORENZA: Joder! [Fuck it all!] Do you want something to drink? Or can I bring you a nice, hot cup of coffee?

RENÉ (*Shaking his head*): No, doña, gracias.

LORENZA: Don't use a foreign language with me, young man. We only speak God's language here. (*RENÉ and SANDRA laugh.*)

RENÉ: Pardón. I mean, excuse me. (*To SANDRA*) What were you saying about your father? Is he here?

SANDRA: I didn't want to tell you on the phone... I thought he'd be here a while and leave.

RENÉ: Is he living with you?

SANDRA: He came three days after you left. And he's still here.

LORENZA: Jodido! [Fucking pest!]

SANDRA: Said he was tired of the country house and all the commotion... And that it was time to be close to me again... in a quiet apartment like this.

LORENZA: And that's when it stopped being quiet.

SANDRA: What could I do? The apartment is his. You couldn't get in because he's installed a metal door. I'll give you a new set of keys. And he's set up a work area in here with two computers, movie and video cameras, amplifiers, sound mixers and I don't know what else.

RENÉ: Rich people and their toys. Right now they're all playing around with their computers, even the babies.

SANDRA: Well, his latest toy is a video he's just shown the two of us.

LORENZA: It's hideous.

SANDRA: And he's not leaving. (*Lowers her voice*) So we're the ones who'll have to go. I've bought an apartment, and it's almost ready to move in. It's nice; you're going to like it! I'll tell him about it soon and we'll go, you and I.

RENÉ: Do you suppose he's come here because he wants to keep an eye on us?

LORENZA: He was already doing that without having to come here.

RENÉ (*Nodding in agreement*): Sandra and I had noticed. But, then why?...

SANDRA: Another of his obsessions.

RENÉ: Or an attempt to separate us.

SANDRA: He knows he can't tell me how to live my life. And I get the feeling that he... really... needs me.

RENÉ (*To LORENZA*): What do you think?

LORENZA: I agree with you both. There's a lot here he needs. And he loves Sandra so much he's lost sight of things.

RENÉ: To the point of giving up his own business?

LORENZA: He never gives up anything.

SANDRA (*Gets up nervously and lights a cigarette*): He assures me he's eager to meet you.

LORENZA: Don't trust him. He's also told her she doesn't need a private tutor.

SANDRA: That was just an offhand comment, Mommy.

LORENZA: It's what he believes. (*All smiles, ALFREDO appears in the doorway, impeccably dressed.*)

ALFREDO: Good morning.

RENÉ: Good morning, sir.

ALFREDO (*Advancing with his hand extended*): So you're René.

RENÉ: Yes, sir. I'm glad to meet you. (*THEY shake hands.*)

ALFREDO: Can I offer you something?

LORENZA: Sir, he doesn't want anything.

ALFREDO: A whiskey never hurt anyone. And I'm going to have one myself. (*To RENÉ*) How about you?

RENÉ: As you wish, sir. (*LORENZA rushes upstage.*)

ALFREDO (*Stopping her with a look*): Don't bother. I'll fix them myself.

SANDRA (*Nervous*): Or I will. I know how you both like them. And I feel like a drink too.

ALFREDO: Thanks, my dear.

LORENZA (*Insulted*): Excuse me. (*To herself*) Tirano! [Tyrant!] (*SHE exits hurriedly right.*)

ALFREDO (*Laughing*): Now she's angry! She's very obliging but she likes to do things her way too. But just think, my poor wife died soon after Sandra was born, and she raised the child.

RENÉ: And that's why you call her "Mommy"...

ALFREDO: Well, it's deserved. She cared for Sandra even when we were living abroad.

RENÉ: I know. She told me, and she has some favorite foreign expressions.

ALFREDO: Probably obscenities. She didn't exactly study the great works of literature, but she picked up a lot in the streets.

RENÉ: So I gathered. Forgive me, sir, but she seems like a character from a play.

ALFREDO: Lorenza?

RENÉ: Yes. How many times have we seen outspoken nurses on the stage? Since the ones in Greek tragedy, there must be more than a hundred. And the fact is they're very real. And always speak their mind.

ALFREDO: That's true! Why do suppose they're like that? (*HE prepares the drinks. SANDRA doesn't miss a word.*)

RENÉ: Perhaps... to compensate for being slaves, and their masters allow it to mask that fact. (*Brief silence*) I'm sorry. I was speaking in generalities.

ALFREDO: But with real insight. Yes, indeed.

SANDRA (*Delighted, to ALFREDO*): Didn't I tell you?

ALFREDO: Sit down, please. We'll be comfortable here. (*Indicates the sofa.*)

RENÉ: Thank you. (*Sits, and ALFREDO sits beside him.*)

ALFREDO: I'll probably get in your way a bit. When I'm not working with my equipment, I like -- I must say -- to spend a little time in this old room I had when I was a child. But you can work in the living room or on the terrace.

RENÉ: Whatever you say, sir.

ALFREDO: No, No! It's up to you. You can have your sessions here if you prefer... (*To SANDRA, who comes over with the three drinks.*) You meet in the afternoon, don't you?

SANDRA: Sometimes in the mornings too. (*Leaves the glasses on the table and sits down.*)

ALFREDO: To your health!

RENÉ: To yours! (*THEY drink.*)

ALFREDO: Do you give any other private lessons?

RENÉ: Yes. It's almost my only means of income.

ALFREDO: But don't you receive some additional funds from your parents?...

RENÉ (*Smiles*): They haven't been able to send me anything for years.

SANDRA: Papa, you know very well what it's like in his country now.

ALFREDO: Of course! Forgive me. It was a stupid thing to say. How did you find things on your trip? Have they improved somewhat?

SANDRA: He was only travelling in this country, Papa.

ALFREDO: Oh, I didn't know! To give other lessons?

RENÉ (*Doubting that it's meant as a joke*): No, sir, To work for my country.

SANDRA: I don't think there's any reason to discuss those things, René.

RENÉ: And why not? I have nothing to hide. Sir, I came to Spain to study when my father could still afford it, before the end of the dictatorship.

ALFREDO: Ours?

RENÉ (*Laughs*): Well, both of them. When ours fell, I offered my services immediately, but they told me I should remain here. And since then I haven't gone back.

ALFREDO: You did the right thing. Life must be very difficult over there. Here, on the other hand...

RENÉ: We do live better here, of course. But that's not why I've stayed.

ALFREDO: I wasn't suggesting it... Will you permit me an indiscreet question? I suspect the answer is "No."

RENÉ: Go ahead.

ALFREDO: Are you a Communist?

SANDRA: Papa!

ALFREDO: Sandra, I have my prejudices! That word doesn't frighten me. Besides, I'm not a political person. Politics are a rip-off. It's enough for me to create wealth and jobs... (*To RENÉ.*) Don't answer if you don't want to. Forgive me for asking.

RENÉ (*Who has sat up straight; seriously*): We would have to clarify first the meaning of that word for you. I'll only say that in my country things had to change, and I'm for that change. Asking what one is or isn't is the most difficult question... Nobody knows down deep what they are.

ALFREDO (*Laughing, HE pats him on the thigh.*): Amazing! That is indeed the great question! I ask myself that every day. What am I? What am I like?

RENÉ: So do I. But that doesn't keep me from acting as if I did know.

ALFREDO: Nor me! (*HE thinks it over as he looks at RENÉ and makes up his mind.*) I'm going to show you something. (*Showing his satisfaction,*

HE gets up and heads for the VCR.) I amuse myself here with my little experiments, you know? Like a child.

SANDRA (*Surprised*): You're going to show him that...?

ALFREDO: Why not? He seems to be able to understand it. (*Pushes the TV to its former spot*) Come over here and sit down! And bring your glass! I want you to see the video I've made. (*SANDRA and RENÉ exchange looks. RENÉ gets up with his glass and crosses to sit in front of the TV screen. SANDRA gets up and moves around uneasily. ALFREDO take the remote control.*) It's not perfect: And it's rather short; I didn't have enough material. With computers and a very good artist I managed to fill in the gaps... Not too much, because I didn't want to falsify reality. But it was necessary to achieve a sense of continuity, even changing the lighting and adjusting the photos, one by one, so they'd appear the same size... A laborious task. Incomplete, of course. The future is missing.

RENÉ: What future?

ALFREDO: Mine, naturally. (*Laughs*) In a moment you'll understand. Sit here, Sandra dear! Don't you want to see it again?

SANDRA (*Coldly*): All right. (*Reluctantly, SHE sits beside RENÉ.*)

ALFREDO: It's like a short play. Or like a strange story, difficult to understand. You are a professor of literature; figure it out if you can. It's the monologue of a single character, but motionless and mute.

RENÉ: Mute?

ALFREDO: And still. These days they make artistic videos of unreal things, full of sounds and movements achieved to perfection. This is just the opposite. The object doesn't move, but it's real. And it changes.

RENÉ: Interesting.

ALFREDO: You think so? My daughter finds it disappointing.

SANDRA: I haven't said that.

ALFREDO: But you think it, and perhaps you're right. It's not much of anything now. But tomorrow... it could be an exciting game for a lot of people. I could even get a patent on it.

RENÉ: Can we see it?

ALFREDO: Indeed! (*HE presses the remote and situates himself behind them. Jokingly*) The curtain rises! (*The lights dim softly and changes to a bluish illumination that seems to emanate from the TV screen, turning their faces pallid, while the room is enveloped in cold semi-darkness. The glow over the courtyard window remains, but is now lunar. THEY speak in subdued tones.*)

RENÉ (*Surprised*): "Time in my Hands"?

ALFREDO: Just to give it a title. (*The three watch.*)

RENÉ: A babe in arms...

SANDRA: My father.

RENÉ: And that date that flashed by?

ALFREDO: The date of my birth. There are several more.

RENÉ: Always just the bust and facing forward.

ALFREDO: And the same size. I've tried to capture the gradual change in the same person.

RENÉ: In you.

ALFREDO: In me.

RENÉ: Wasn't there a slight leap in time?

ALFREDO: It's not the only one. The continuity wasn't easy. Not even with the help of my sketcher, because I didn't want to lie. At times I keep the same photogram for several seconds, so that the video won't be too short. (*Pause. THEY watch.*) You see? In the lower corner, the number fourteen. Fourteen years old. (*Faint and distant, the notes of the allegro of Brahms' Quintet in B Minor for clarinet and strings begin.*)

ALFREDO: That good music again...

RENÉ: Sometimes we hear it coming from somewhere in the neighborhood. Don't we, Sandra?

SANDRA: Yes.

RENÉ (*To ALFREDO*): Or is it on the tape?

ALFREDO: No. It's coming from the courtyard.

RENÉ: More numbers.

ALFREDO: I can stop where I please. (*Presses the remote*) You see? And go back. Or vary the speed. (*Jovially*) Time in my hands!

RENÉ: Go on, please. (*ALFREDO presses the remote button.*)

ALFREDO (*After a few moments*): Do you get it? It's like those films where we see the growth of a flower into full blossom in only a few moments.

RENÉ: Or watch it close its petals again.

ALFREDO: That's right! I'm not moving there but my features are changing rapidly. An entire life compressed into a few moments. (*SANDRA gets up brusquely.*)

SANDRA: Excuse me. (*Under her father's cheerful look, SHE opts to justify her flight from the video by filling her glass again. Then SHE drinks with a show of discomfort.*)

ALFREDO: I'm tiring you out. I'll speed it up. (*Presses the remote*) The years fly by... The wrinkles increase... (*Brief pause*) And the end! (*HE turns off the set.*) For now, of course. (*HE leaves the remote on the TV.*

The light returns slowly to its former level. The music goes on.) More whiskey?

RENÉ (*In thought, still seated*): No, thanks. (*ALFREDO takes his glass from the table and drinks a little.*)

ALFREDO: What did you think of it? (*SANDRA shifts her position and lights another cigarette.*)

RENÉ: The continuity is very smooth... It becomes quite impressive.

ALFREDO: Truly? (*To SANDRA*) You smoke too much, dear. You should cut back on those cigarettes. (*SHE reacts with a slight grunt and blows another vigorous puff of smoke.*)

RENÉ: How did you get the idea for this experiment?

ALFREDO (*Going over to RENÉ*): I don't know. It was just a distraction.

RENÉ: When we were talking about not knowing what we're really like, you wanted to show it to me. Are you trying to know yourself better through the video?

ALFREDO: I'm not sure what I'm trying to do... I suppose that when I stop it at one age or another, it will help me to remember.

RENÉ: And when you rewind it?

ALFREDO: What do you mean?

RENÉ (*Gets up slowly*): You are a man of action, and the future has probably meant more to you than the past. And now, do you want to go backwards?

ALFREDO (*Looks at him fixedly*): A man of action also reconsiders the past in order to progress better. And the video also runs forward. And at my will! So, what do you think?

RENÉ (*Cautiously*): Yes, you're right. Time in your hands. And at the same time, the desire to recapture your youth. (*Smiles*) I'll have to give it all some thought.

ALFREDO (*Laughs*): So will I! But I like what you say. Have another drink my friend!

SANDRA: You can have mine, if you wish. (*Offers it to him*) I don't care for it. (*RENÉ takes it mechanically.*)

ALFREDO (*Taking it away from him; affably*): Give him another, dear. It's dirty.

SANDRA: There's no danger. We're both healthy. (*Suggestively*) And we do it often.

RENÉ: But Sandra, your father...

ALFREDO (*All smiles*): Your father understands everything... including the ways of youth. (*HE sits again on the sofa.*)

SANDRA (*Confronting him*): Well, you still have a few things to learn about us.

RENÉ: Sandra, do you think this is the time...?

SANDRA: Why not?

ALFREDO (*Quickly*): You can tell me later. Assuming I don't already know... Right now I'm more interested in hearing what your professor has to say. I find it worthwhile. (*SANDRA steps away, annoyed.*) You were talking about my getting even more control over my life... (*With a stubborn look, SANDRA sits on the sofa, as far as possible from her father. The music fades away softly.*)

RENÉ: No, you were saying that.

ALFREDO: It's true. I was the one! (*HE breaks off and listens.*) You can't hear the music anymore.

SANDRA: No.

ALFREDO: And you, my young friend, what else can you tell me?

RENÉ (*Takes a sip walks about*): One thing I've observed. We all want to preserve our likenesses. Our past. Don't let it vanish! And older men of action are the ones who work at it most. It has to do with ego.

ALFREDO: Did you say ego?

RENÉ: Yes. From the time of the pharaohs, no less. Later, kings and business magnates commission their portraits in oil.

ALFREDO: Vanity... or ego, as you say. I'm certainly not lacking that either.

RENÉ (*Looks at him*): Then photography comes along and we can all have our pictures taken, endlessly. We perpetuate ourselves not only in our children but in photographs.

ALFREDO: It's as if we were converting the world into one vast archive.

RENÉ: Right. But movement was missing, so we invent the motion picture. An improved way to fight against death.

ALFREDO: How's that?

RENÉ: Yes. To keep ourselves alive, talking and moving, since we inevitably will disappear. And now comes the best of all. You stop and manipulate time itself... backwards and forward... to better process your life. And you create an unforeseen mirror.

ALFREDO (*After a moment*): I like your professor, Sandra! (*To RENÉ*) I'd be delighted to go on talking about this, and other things... Since you're going to be coming here regularly...

SANDRA (*Determined*): No, Papa.

ALFREDO: What do you mean "no"?

SANDRA: I'm going to move to an apartment I've bought. (*Tense silence*)

ALFREDO: I'm sorry to hear that. I need you here with me, more than you imagine.

SANDRA (*Gets up, angry*): I'm sorry, Papa, but you have your life and I have mine! I left the country place, and I'll leave here too.

ALFREDO (*Weakly*): Soon?

SANDRA: In a week or so.

ALFREDO: Is it so difficult for you to live with me?

SANDRA: Papa, it's not that. You don't understand anything!

ALFREDO: You give her some advice, René... She's safer here...

RENÉ: Sir, it's not my place to advise her.

ALFREDO (*To SANDRA*): Have you installed burglar alarms in that other apartment?

SANDRA: But don't you understand? That's exactly what I'm trying to escape from. And from your dreadfully boring social events, and from all those creeps you bring up as possible husbands, and from your bodyguards. You'll end up putting bars on all the windows for sure. But you're not going to lock me up behind those bars!

ALFREDO: We all have to protect you. You too, René.

SANDRA: No! That way you mark me even more. There goes the daughter of that very rich executive, followed by his thugs. I can't put up with that. With you or away from you, that's not going to be my life. And if I have to go even farther, I will. (*Uncomfortable pause*)

ALFREDO: This city is bustling with dangers, Sandra.

SANDRA (*Sarcastically*): What are you afraid of? That they'll kidnap me? Rape me?

ALFREDO (*Hesitant*): As a start.

SANDRA: Are you afraid I'll turn to drugs?

ALFREDO (*Suddenly excited*): I never said that!

SANDRA: Don't worry! I know what I'm doing. (*Brief pause*) Don't waste your energy, Papa. I'm leaving.

ALFREDO: You've been on edge... You could take a cruise on the yacht, invite your friends if you wish.

SANDRA: Another jail.

ALFREDO: Think about it.

SANDRA: I already have. (*Silence. With his flashy leather briefcase in hand, JAVIER appears in the doorway and stops.*)

JAVIER: Good morning.

SANDRA: Hello, Javi. (*ALFREDO gets up and SHE steps aside, as if putting an end to the argument with her father.*)

ALFREDO: Hello, son! I'm not sure if you know...

JAVIER: Only by sight. (*Steps forward with outstretched hand*) You're my sister's tutor. A pleasure to meet you.

RENÉ: The pleasure's mine. (*THEY shake hands.*) You must excuse me... I have another class, and I'm going to be late. (*HE goes to get his briefcase and opens it.*) I'll leave the Rabelais video for you, Sandra. (*Takes it out and leaves it on the table. To ALFREDO*) Sir, my pleasure.

ALFREDO (*Taking his hand*): Come back whenever you like! We must continue our discussion about... that whim of mine.

RENÉ (*To SANDRA*): This evening, at the usual time?

SANDRA: Of course. But I'm leaving with you now. I'll take you in the car. Good-bye, Papa. Good-bye, Javi.

JAVIER: Hey, don't be so rude. Aren't you going to give your brother a kiss? (*SANDRA smiles without enthusiasm, and as SHE passes by him, SHE allows him a routine kiss. RENÉ, who is waiting for her in the doorway, takes his leave with a slight bow. They exit together. JAVIER opens his briefcase, takes out a newspaper which he leaves at one side and a folder that he places on the table.*) Were you having an argument?

ALFREDO (*HE has gone to the window and is looking out into the courtyard.*): You know how Sandra is. She just told me that she's moving to an apartment she's found. (*Doubtlessly already aware of the apartment, JAVIER nods and starts to say something.*) One moment... (*HE touches two or three buttons on the telephone and picks up.*) My daughter has just left. Keep an eye on her.

JAVIER: You shouldn't have come here.

ALFREDO: She's our girl, Javier. And we must watch over her.

JAVIER: We were already doing that.

ALFREDO: But closer.

JAVIER: If she's not being careful...

ALFREDO: Things have gotten serious. You know that she's very independent and never got involved in love affairs. This time the reports are all in agreement: she's head over heels in love. Being the way she is, I suspect this is the real thing. Her first and maybe only love. I can understand it; he's intelligent and likeable.

JAVIER: He's a fortune hunter disguised as an idealist. That's for sure! (*Looks at his watch*) What whim of yours were you discussing with him?

ALFREDO: Huh?... Oh, a video I've been working on.

JAVIER: You could amuse yourself more with your business affairs.

ALFREDO: I'm not neglecting them.

JAVIER: Thanks to me.

ALFREDO: It's your turn, son. They bore me a little now.

JAVIER (*Walks about, annoyed*): But you're still in charge. And everyday there are decisions to make.

ALFREDO: You'll bring me anything I have to sign. Let's see now... (*HE sits at the table and begins to sign papers.*)

JAVIER: It's not enough just to sign. There are strategies to be considered.

ALFREDO: And we do that.

JAVIER: Yes? Even for dealing with family matters? Have you thought of a way to break up that relationship between René and Sandra? I suppose that's what you want...

ALFREDO: We must act carefully. And try not to hurt her.

JAVIER: We could get him thrown out of Spain. There's no lack of pretexts: he's a political activist, an agitator.

ALFREDO: Only for his own country.

JAVIER: An activist is always dangerous.

ALFREDO: No, no. It would be a mistake to expel him.

JAVIER: Why?

ALFREDO: Because Sandra might follow him. And that must be avoided.

JAVIER: To his country?

ALFREDO: Or some other.

JAVIER: Not to his. She knows how bad she'd have it there and she's not that crazy.

ALFREDO: I don't think you know your sister. (*HE closes the folder.*) Fine. Everything is in order. Here. (*HE hands it to JAVIER who places it in his briefcase. ALFREDO gets up and returns to the window.*) Javier, this thing with René has affected Sandra very deeply. It's no passing fancy. That's quite clear.

JAVIER: Then if it's so serious, maybe it would work better if we got him to leave voluntarily. Let him break up with her! And that way she wouldn't be able to follow him.

ALFREDO (*Skeptically*): Just tell me how.

JAVIER: With an offer.

ALFREDO: (*Surprised, HE goes closer to him.*): Of money?

JAVIER: In comparison with the fortune that Sandra will inherit someday, an insignificant amount, but attractive for him since a bird in the hand is worth more.

ALFREDO (*Sits down, doubtful*): It needs thought. It could be counterproductive.

JAVIER: Papa, you always play it cautious. If the matter is urgent, let me do it my way. There's nobody who can't be bought. Especially for a few million.

ALFREDO: What?

JAVIER: A trifle for us -- which can save our girl from a rash act that can't be undone. I'll dream up an honorable motive.

ALFREDO: I don't like it. It seems rather crude.

JAVIER: I know his type better than you. Will you let me do it? (*Brief pause*) There's no time to waste, because you can be sure they've already slept together.

ALFREDO: You think so?

JAVIER: And so do you. These days young people don't end up in bed; they start off in bed.

ALFREDO: I find the thought repugnant.

JAVIER: So do I. Good reason to proceed without resorting to harsher measures...

ALFREDO: Watch it! We aren't criminals.

JAVIER: Of course not. We'll just break them up cleanly, and the sooner the better.

ALFREDO (*Doubtful*): You'd better give it careful thought. How are you going to broach the subject?

JAVIER: Don't worry. Trust me. By the way, are you going to put bars on the windows?

ALFREDO: It may not be necessary. I've had alarms installed. (*HE goes to the window and peeks out.*)

JAVIER (*With a sigh of annoyance as HE goes to the table*): You should go back to the country!

ALFREDO: As long as Sandra doesn't go, no. (*Smiles*) And maybe not even if she does... I'm beginning to like it here.

JAVIER (*Closes his briefcase*): Don't miss the board meeting at the bank tomorrow. There has to be a thorough discussion of how we're going to participate in the branch that American company is opening here.

ALFREDO: I'll go, I'll go... Is that everything?

JAVIER (*Leaves his briefcase in order and turns to face him*): No. I suppose you've read the papers.

ALFREDO (*Contrite*): I've been so busy I...

JAVIER: That does it! (*Picks up the newspaper he left on the table*) Here it is. (*Flips through pages*) Read this. (*Points. ALFREDO frowns and reads.*) It's about Mundifisa.

ALFREDO: What are they going to do? An audit?

JAVIER: More. A special investigation. And probably a trial.

ALFREDO: But it's only a corporation for investments and financing!

JAVIER: An international cartel.

ALFREDO: Like a lot of others. Reason enough for them to act prudently. We've only put money into it. The funds end up in a variety of places; they manage innumerable businesses around the world...

JAVIER: And among them, the one that's singled out here. But they were giving 17 to 18 percent interest; the newspapers have got wind of everything and joined the hunt.

ALFREDO (*Walks about in thought*): How much have we invested in it?

JAVIER: You know perfectly well. Millions.

ALFREDO: There are larger investors. And some that are very influential... one of whom assured me there would be no problems.

JAVIER: Well, now you see that there are.

ALFREDO: You think it's serious?

JAVIER: I suppose not for us. Mundifisa handled its books very well and those earnings are off the books... Still, it says here that the CEO in Spain has left the country.

ALFREDO (*Annoyed*): I've read it.

JAVIER: Maybe they'll ask the major investors to testify. Why don't you take a trip yourself? There's no lack of business to attend to abroad.

ALFREDO: Now? That would be self-incrimination. Do you really think Mundifisa was financing that business?

JAVIER: (*Astounded*): Are you going to pretend with me? You carried out that operation yourself. Don't tell me you weren't informed. Leave that for the prosecutor, if he calls us.

ALFREDO (*Angered, HE throws the newspaper on the table. His tone is not convincing.*): No! It never entered my mind and I didn't check it out.

JAVIER: You, the ever cautious one? I don't believe it.

ALFREDO (*Changes his tone*): It's true... in part. But I was given assurances.

JAVIER: Well, you'd better be on your guard. (*LORENZA enters.*)

ALFREDO: I'll make some calls.

JAVIER: It'll be better if you go in person. I'll keep you informed. (*Looks at his watch and picks up his briefcase*) See you tomorrow at the bank.

LORENZA: Excuse me, sir. (*To ALFREDO*) Are you going to eat here?

ALFREDO: What?... yes.

LORENZA (*To JAVIER*): Do you want to stay and eat too?

JAVIER: No, thanks. I'll be on my way. (*HE begins his exit.*)

LORENZA: Good-bye.

JAVIER (*Stopping*): By the way, Mommy... was professor René in the habit of sleeping over here?

ALFREDO: Javier!

JAVIER: Speak up, Mommy.

LORENZA (*Evading his meaning*): Sleeping... over?

JAVIER: Yes, Mommy. Spending the night.

LORENZA (*Embarrassed*): Professor René has his own place...

JAVIER: But did he sleep here some nights? There's a guest room...

LORENZA: I... don't know. Sometimes they'd work very late and I'd go to bed. Ask your sister.

JAVIER: (*Ironically*): Sure. Papa, I'll see you tomorrow. (*Exits*)

LORENZA (*Starts to leave in turn*): If there's nothing you need...

ALFREDO: Mommy, if Sandra was having an affair with that man before I moved in here, you should have informed me. Was she?

LORENZA (*Hesitates*): I don't know. I never speak of those things. (*SHE is silent a moment.*) You know that I never speak of those things.

ALFREDO (*Looking away*): I'm sorry.

LORENZA: Excuse me. (*SHE picks up the used glasses.*) I'll be back with clean ones. (*SHE exits. Deep in thought, ALFREDO doesn't move. The adagio of Brahms' Quintet for clarinet and strings begins very faintly. ALFREDO looks up and goes to the window to look out. HE sighs and goes over to the VCR, takes the remote, turns on the TV set and sits in front of it. The light dims a bit and becomes strange again.*)

ALFREDO (*In a low voice*): Forty... thirty-five... twenty years old. (*HE stops the tape and observes his face from the past. Without the slightest sound, the window in the courtyard is opened by a pretty young girl of sixteen, dressed in inexpensive old-fashioned clothes. After glancing at ALFREDO's window, SHE sits near the open window and begins to sew. The music grows a bit louder. Without turning around, ALFREDO looks up and becomes lost in memory. A few seconds pass. LORENZA returns with clean glasses on a tray and goes to place them on the bar. Without any movement from the girl in the window, the shutters turn silently and close by themselves. The music continues softly, but the light returns to normal. ALFREDO reacts and turns off the video.*) Is the window open, Lorenza?

LORENZA: Which window?

ALFREDO: Which one do you think? This one.

LORENZA: No.

ALFREDO: Is there another one open somewhere?

LORENZA: Where do you mean?

ALFREDO: I don't know... The one in the courtyard... You can hear the music from the neighbor's apartment.

LORENZA: When you were a boy you couldn't bear it.

ALFREDO: Really?

LORENZA: Don't you remember?

ALFREDO: So many things are forgotten...

LORENZA: It was the neighbor's daughter. Her father bought her a gramophone; that's how the girl got interested in music. Hearing those wisps of music for more than forty years... You must have been ten when it started.

ALFREDO: Yes. That's true. A girl would appear at times in the window... (*HE gets up and goes to her side to look at out.*)

LORENZA (*Nods in agreement*): And she would sit down and sew. But her father died, and then the mother passed away a few years ago. And she keeps on taking in sewing and playing her records... But she never comes to the window now. You've probably noticed.

ALFREDO: I hadn't realized...

LORENZA (*With a cold smile*): Don't you remember her name either?

ALFREDO: Her name?

LORENZA: Her name came up in this house a few times... Isolina Sánchez. (*SHE looks at him. HE avoids her eyes.*) She's probably sewing this minute behind the shutters.

ALFREDO: Maybe she is.

LORENZA (*Dryly*): But now, it's as if she weren't there at all. (*SHE steps away and exits rapidly with tray in hand. Very unnerved, ALFREDO watches her leave. The light begins to dim until the room is submerged in darkness. The girl's window darkens in turn and, immediately, the entire courtyard. The music fades as at stage left a cold brightness grows and quickly spreads over the downstage area. The wall graph shines behind the simple furnishings. JAVIER is seated on the small sofa. RENÉ enters from downstage right, crosses, and ends up near JAVIER, who gets up smiling. THEY shake hands.*)

JAVIER: Thanks for coming. Sit down, please. What would you like to drink?

RENÉ: Nothing for the moment, thank you. (*THEY both sit down.*)

JAVIER: It's a delicate matter and I'm counting on your discretion.

RENÉ: I'm listening.

JAVIER: You're not unaware that our government is rather favorable toward your country.

RENÉ: And we're very grateful.

JAVIER: I'm not going to pretend with you. I won't hide the fact that personally I have no sympathy for your cause.

RENÉ (*Smiles*): I must say I'd be surprised if you did.

JAVIER: I'm not trying to provoke you. I only want to keep things clear between us. You'll admit that your people are living under a dictatorship, and deplorable violations of human rights are being committed.

RENÉ: That may well be. And where is that not happening? But I don't recall that the social forces you represent protested the violations of human rights committed in my country, year after year, under the long and harsh dictatorship of our former president. Besides, if you visited us, you'd see that there's more freedom and political pluralism than you imagine.

JAVIER (*Laughs*): Perfect. Each of us with his opinion. But mine is of the least concern now; it's the assets of our bank that matter. And following the criteria of our government we have considered, like any other financial entity, helping you. (*Surprise from RENÉ*) It will not be an operation just for show; its aims are different. We don't expect the public gratitude of your country's government or even written justification for this aid.

RENÉ: I confess I don't understand.

JAVIER: No signature; no declaration. Only the word of a person of trust. And you can be trusted.

RENÉ: Thank you.

JAVIER: So you see, in spite of everything, our position is not so inflexible.

RENÉ: Whose position?

JAVIER: My bank's... And the social group to which I belong. Some of them, at least.

RENÉ: No doubt you have your reasons. But in certain other countries, it's your kind who're funding the rebels who are fighting us.

JAVIER: Fine. But let's not argue over a complex situation. Would your government accept a contribution without publicity?

RENÉ: Why without publicity?

JAVIER: Precisely not to upset a lot of people who wouldn't approve.

RENÉ: High level politics!

JAVIER: If you want to call it that. But we aren't involved in politics.

RENÉ (*Thinking*): I suppose my country would accept contributions without publicity, depending on what it would have to give in return. But I lack authority to give you an answer.

JAVIER: Nevertheless, you have the right to receive whatever people give you for it. Without signatures or written proof. You've been selected because you're discreet and honest. (*RENÉ is looking at him very intrigued.*) Do you really not want to take anything?

RENÉ: No, thanks.

JAVIER: The amount would be modest. At the present time it can't be larger. We would open an account in your name at our Paris branch for four hundred thousand dollars.

RENÉ: With no formal agreement?

JAVIER: Exactly.

RENÉ: For me to hand over to my country?

JAVIER: In whatever manner you prefer. You could transfer the money or turn it over to your ambassador in Paris, for example. The account would be set up so that you could draw on it freely, and it would be carried out with the utmost discretion outside Spain. And you and I would not see each other again. (*Silence. RENÉ begins to laugh softly. JAVIER smiles.*)

RENÉ: The only condition: that I say good-bye to... all my friends here and that I not return to Spain. Am I wrong?

JAVIER: How can that matter if you have to return to your country sooner or later? Do it now.

RENÉ: Suppose I don't hand over that money to my government...

JAVIER: We'll take that risk. In any case, you're the best emissary.

RENÉ: I never thought my price would be so high. Why don't you save your money? You could use your influence to force me out of Spain without spending a dollar. Isn't that what you're really up to?

JAVIER: Who said anything about a price? It's simply a matter of contributing to your country.

RENÉ (*Gets up*): It's a matter of my leaving voluntarily. (*JAVIER starts to speak.*) Please! Don't insult my intelligence by repeating that incredible offer. (*JAVIER gets up in turn, tense.*)

JAVIER: Do you mean that you don't accept and that you're staying?

RENÉ: Of course. Good day. (*HE starts to leave. JAVIER stops him with a gesture and indicates HE should sit down again.*)

JAVIER: Don't go yet.

RENÉ: It's useless. I...

JAVIER: Please. (*RENÉ doesn't sit down.*) All right. As you wish. (*HE begins a short stroll downstage.*) Your country desperately needs any kind of help, no matter how small. You know that quite well. Among other things you are engaged in collecting funds for it. (*HE advances right and a spot follows him. HE turns around.*) Haven't you considered that you could really hand over the amount I'm offering?

RENÉ: That's not why you're offering it.

JAVIER (*Slowly*): You're the one who must decide whether you accept the money for your cause or reject it. Whether or not they say: "René refused a large amount for his people because he wouldn't accept the small sacrifice of leaving Spain forever."

RENÉ (*Nervous, takes a few steps toward him*): How do I know you won't freeze that account once I've left?

JAVIER (*Ironic*): Haven't you got the point? You are a man of your word, and you'll keep it not to return. And we'll keep ours. If we froze the account, you would consider yourself free to return or to resume your... friendly relations... with any person who went to visit you, even though you had broken off with them. (*HE goes over to RENÉ and gives him a pat on the shoulder.*) We won't cancel the gift. Whether you appropriate it for yourself or give it to your government is your affair. The offer stands. (*HE crosses left. RENÉ goes to center stage and looks straight ahead, very angry.*)

RENÉ: I also have the right to my own feelings... to keep my good name in the eyes of others...

JAVIER (*Smoothly*): Rights that are very beautiful and very... human. You will decide if you prefer exercising those individual rights to fulfilling your patriotic duty. I'll wait a few days for your decision.

RENÉ: There's nothing for you to wait for. Good day. (*HE walks toward the right.*)

JAVIER: Good day to you. (*HE goes left and the two exit on opposite sides. Again, we hear the distant echoes of Brahms' adagio. Lights down on the left and the central area is lit. The TV and VCR are again pushed to the left. SANDRA is sitting in one of the side chairs reading a newspaper. With hands behind his back, her father is looking out the window. The music ceases little by little. ALFREDO goes to the VCR.*)

ALFREDO: Have you removed my cassette?

SANDRA: We had to look at another tape yesterday. Yours is on top of the TV. (*SHE points. ALFREDO puts it in the VCR and turns on the set.*)

SANDRA (*Reading*): How awful!

ALFREDO: What?

SANDRA: Eighteen addicts dead from overdoses of heroin.

ALFREDO (*Puts down the remote*): That's the world we live in.

SANDRA: Then something has to be done to change it.

ALFREDO: In what way?

SANDRA: Couldn't those of you who are really powerful do something?

ALFREDO: The western governments are already doing a lot, dear. They're capturing more and more traffickers all over the world. (*LORENZA appears at the door.*)
SANDRA: But they never get the ones at the top! (*A silence that LORENZA interrupts.*)
LORENZA: Coffee or tea for you, sir?
ALFREDO: Nothing, Mommy. Thanks. I have to go out. (*HE moves away from the set and lights a cigarette.*)
SANDRA (*In response to a look from LORENZA*): I don't want anything now either. Wait until René comes. (*LORENZA starts to leave.*) But don't go! (*Points to a magazine on the table*) Look at the two pages I've turned down in Vogue and tell me which dress you like best. (*LORENZA sits by the table and leafs through the magazine. SANDRA leaves the newspaper on the chair and goes over to LORENZA. ALFREDO hesitates a second, takes the paper, sits down and glances over it with affected indifference.*)
SANDRA (*Beside LORENZA, SHE leans over and points.*): Do you see them, Mommy? I'm crazy about the blue one. Don't you think it's out of this world?
LORENZA: Yes, it's pretty. But I like the pearl grey. (*ALFREDO laughs affably.*)
SANDRA: Are you laughing at us?
ALFREDO: From pure pleasure, my dear. After reading all the terrible things in the paper, it delights me to think how good it is to protect our children so that they can live a good life and even buy the dress they fancy.
SANDRA: I have no intention of buying it.
ALFREDO: (*Amazed*): Why not?
SANDRA: You don't understand at all, Papa. I'm going to hire a dressmaker to make me a copy.
ALFREDO: Why, if you can get the one you want?
SANDRA: To avoid wasting money, to live simply... (*Laughs*) And to make a few changes of my own in the design.
LORENZA: Indeed, that's the way we ought to live.
ALFREDO: You already have your blue jeans for the simple life.
SANDRA: And I used to have a dressmaker who did very good work for me.
ALFREDO: Well, I think you want the same as Picasso: to have a lot of money in order to live like a poor man.
LORENZA (*Agreeing*): Clever fellow.

ALFREDO: More than I, no doubt. But I can't wear blue jeans.

SANDRA: Then you're missing out.

ALFREDO: I've missed out so that you won't miss out on anything, whether it's an expensive dress or blue jeans... Live the way you please, dear.

SANDRA: That's what I'm doing. My only problem is I lost my dressmaker. She got married.

LORENZA: There are others around... There is a very good one who lives close by. (*ALFREDO looks at her in surprise.*)

SANDRA: Then I'll give her a call. Who is she?

LORENZA: You must have seen her at one time or another in the window across the way. The one the music comes from. (*ALFREDO sits, astonished.*)

SANDRA: I don't recall.

LORENZA: Well, she's spent her whole life sewing behind that window. Hasn't she, sir?

ALFREDO: Yes... I do think I've seen her.

LORENZA: Her name is Isolina Sánchez. If you wish, I'll call her for you.

SANDRA: When I move to the other apartment. It won't be long now. (*Lights up at left. JAVIER enters, picks up the phone and begins to dial.*)

ALFREDO (*Gets up and walks about*): Do you insist on leaving me?

SANDRA: Didn't you come to this apartment? Well, I'm going to another.

ALFREDO: I feel tired, Sandra. I needed a family, and you are my family.

SANDRA: I'm tired too... of your bodyguards.

ALFREDO: If you stayed, I'd respect your schedule. And you could have this room for your classes. I'm ready to make concessions.

SANDRA: Papa, I'm the one who's making concessions. (*ALFREDO is about to answer, but the telephone rings.*)

ALFREDO: It's probably for me... (*Picks up*) Hello.

JAVIER: Papa, I must insist again that you come back to the office. We need you, and don't use the excuse about being tired.

ALFREDO: Well, I am. What's going on now? If you call me, there must be a reason.

JAVIER: Pay attention to what I'm saying and what I'm not saying. It's likely there'll be subpoenas. There are sums whose depositors don't know where they end up, as happens with those in the banks. (*SANDRA and LORENZA look at dress illustrations in the magazine.*)

ALFREDO: In theory, fine. But with the larger investments, no one's going to think that.

JAVIER (*With pointed irony*): Oh, no?... Well, you yourself told me you didn't know where they'd end up. But it's all the same, if there are no sworn depositions required.

ALFREDO: This afternoon I'll be seeing someone... you already know who...

JAVIER: Perfect. It will facilitate matters. Our newspaper chain already has instructions, and our attorneys are at work.

ALFREDO: Fine. Is that all?

JAVIER: Well, I've had a talk with our little professor.

ALFREDO (*Looking at his daughter*): Ah!

LORENZA: Professor René won't be long. I'll fix some...

SANDRA: Wait! Look at this one. (*THEY turn pages. ALFREDO signals them to lower their voices.*)

JAVIER: I'm sorry to say that, in principle, he rejects the offer.

ALFREDO: Then I was right!

JAVIER: At the moment he aspires to much more because he thinks he has her in his pocket. But I believe he'll give it some thought. And if he persists in refusing, we can always...

ALFREDO: No. Leave that to me. I've already come up with a way to resolve it. A way that will surprise you. (*SANDRA looks at him with a hint of suspicion.*)

JAVIER: What is it?

ALFREDO (*Laughs*): You'll see. And I'll hear no objections!

JAVIER: I'm afraid of what you've decided.

ALFREDO: Good bye. (*HE hangs up. In thought, JAVIER exits left and the area grows dark.*)

SANDRA (*To LORENZA*): Then it's going to be the blue one?

LORENZA: If you've already decided then why ask? (*A little laugh from SANDRA*) I'm going to the kitchen. (*LORENZA gets up and as she crosses to the door, she murmurs.*) Stubborn as a mule.

ALFREDO (*Laughs*): Why not say it in your other language, Mommy?

LORENZA: With her there's no need. (*Exits*)

SANDRA (*Holds up the magazine*): Do you like it, Papa?

ALFREDO (*Goes near the window and looks at the one across the way*): You like it and that's what counts. (*SANDRA closes the magazine with a smile. ALFREDO risks some timid words.*) Listen, dear... Has Mommy Lorenza never spoken to you about that young woman in the apartment across the way?

SANDRA: I don't think so...

ALFREDO: She will. She's already begun. Don't you remember her? (*Intrigued, SANDRA shakes her head.*) I do. I saw her often.

SANDRA: And you probably even talked with her, didn't you? (*Smiling*) You were something!

ALFREDO: We never exchanged a word.

SANDRA (*SHE gets up and goes toward him.*): Don't lie to me. Was she perhaps... one of your conquests?

ALFREDO: What conquests are you talking about?

SANDRA: Don't pretend. It's obvious to me that you had them. I know that you and Mama didn't get along. (*SHE smiles. ALFREDO steps away and sits in an easy chair.*) Don't think I'm blaming you... I know that she was always going to parties and having her own fun...

ALFREDO: You know it from Lorenza, of course.

SANDRA: And from others.

ALFREDO: From Lorenza, who's been a real mother to you. (*Pensive*) What I don't understand is why she wants to bring that woman here.

SANDRA: Relax. Mommy will speak with her over there.

ALFREDO (*Shakes his head*): Mommy Lorenza wants to bring her here.

SANDRA: Because she's a dressmaker.

ALFREDO (*After a moment*): Come over here. Sit beside me. (*HE pats the chair next to him. Intrigued, SANDRA sits beside him.*) I'm going to tell you something. It's for you alone.

SANDRA: About the dressmaker?

ALFREDO: In a way...

SANDRA: Did you know her?

ALFREDO: I've already told you I didn't... I loved your mother very much, or I believed that I loved her. But it wasn't real love. We got married because our families were friends, because I liked her very much... We soon grew apart. And I... had my affairs.

SANDRA: And she had hers. You're not telling me anything new.

ALFREDO: Did you learn that from Mommy too?

SANDRA: Whom else?

ALFREDO (*Bothered*): She'll say no doubt that she never speaks of those things. Sandra, maybe she wasn't a good mother to Javier or a good wife for me because I failed to be a good husband... You must forgive both of us.

SANDRA (*coldly*): I have nothing to forgive. And at this point you shouldn't worry about it.

ALFREDO: I can't help it. Because I did feel true love. Once! And I never... dared try to do anything about it. Would you like to know?

SANDRA (*A fleeting glance at the window*): Is it possible?...

ALFREDO: I must have been nine or ten when I saw her for the first time.

SANDRA: From this window?

ALFREDO (*Nods*): A beautiful little girl of six or seven. Who says a blind passion isn't possible at that age? The body hasn't matured but our feelings have. I saw her and I could think of no one else. She hadn't started sewing. She would sit at her window and play with her doll, while she listened, while we listened, to the music her father played on the gramophone.

SANDRA: And which she keeps on playing!

ALFREDO: From time to time she would give me a quick look that made me tremble all over. I want to believe that it was more than flirting, that she also loved me a little... (*The memory excites him.*) Once days passed and she didn't appear at the window. I was about to go crazy. Then, one night, during dinner, I hear my father say: It seems that the Sánchez girl has scarlet fever and she's very ill. I thought I'd die! I managed to hide my anxiety, I looked up scarlet fever in the dictionary, I prayed, and I cried in my bed... And still that was... happiness! Maybe you don't understand.

SANDRA: I do understand.

ALFREDO: Finally she appeared again, showing the effects of her illness... And from this window I saw her grow up in hers and turn into an adorable woman.

SANDRA: All those years?

ALFREDO: Until I was twenty-eight and we moved to the country place. She was probably twenty-five then. I got married the next year. (*HE becomes silent.*)

SANDRA: And in all those years... you didn't dare to say anything to her or look for her?

ALFREDO: Never.

SANDRA: But you've always been so confident...

ALFREDO: With others. Not with her.

SANDRA (*After a moment*): Are you saying that you haven't come back here to live with me or watch over me but because of her?

ALFREDO: For you too. You're what I love most...

SANDRA: And for her.

ALFREDO: Yes. (*SANDRA gets up and presses his shoulder. SHE takes a cigarette from the box and lights it. SHE takes a few hesitant steps, stops and looks at him fixedly.*) My dear, I would still like to realize my dream. To live with you and maybe, maybe... with her.

SANDRA (*Mumbles*): What?

ALFREDO (*Rapid glance at the VCR*): To rescue the best of the time that's gone. To be a child again, and a boy... to erase bitterness... Yes, I know. I'm a powerful executive who hasn't lacked satisfactions and beautiful women friends... And what's left of all that? Nothing! (*HE touches his chest.*) Here inside only you remain (*Slight gesture upstage*) And her. Isolina. Will you help me dream that dream?

SANDRA: Have you seen her again?

ALFREDO: I know she's behind the curtains when I hear her music. But she doesn't come to the window.

SANDRA: She must be a lot older now.

ALFREDO: I'd guess fifty-three. It's ridiculous, I know! But... what if she's been waiting for me all her life? Calling me timidly, year after year, with her music? Trying to keep herself attractive... These days it's not so difficult at her age. (*HE gets up and goes toward the window.*) If one day she opens the window, I'll speak to her.

SANDRA: And if she doesn't?

ALFREDO: I'll wait at her door. I'll approach her.

SANDRA: Are you thinking... of marrying again?

ALFREDO: Would that matter to you? May be she could come to be a kind of friend for you... (*HE is silent, with a pleading look.*)

SANDRA: I don't know what to say to you, Papa... It all seems so... improbable...

ALFREDO: Don't you dream of something that you also think is improbable? I'd like to believe that that woman... that music, so distant and yet so near... will one day be mine. Will it?... (*Disturbed, SANDRA smokes and walks about.*) Let this stay between you and me.

SANDRA: Don't worry.

ALFREDO (*Goes to her side and kisses her hair*): Do you want us to realize my dream together... and yours?

SANDRA (*Her voice trembles*): Mine?

ALFREDO: Don't move to another apartment. I can be understanding.

SANDRA (*Stepping away a little*): Papa, please...

ALFREDO: All of us together. My dream will not be complete if you are missing from it, Now it's a nightmare.

SANDRA: Why a nightmare? (*Softly, the Funeral March from Beethoven's Third Symphony, the Eroica, begins; it is not certain that it's coming from the courtyard, whose light remains unchanging. But in the room, invaded by spreading semi-darkness, the light begins to oscillate over the faces of the father and daughter with pronounced fluctuations. The voice of ALFREDO and SANDRA sound tense and murmuring although without emphasis.*)

ALFREDO: A nightmare that returns some nights, in which you say good-bye to me. I look for you, as I came here to look for you, and you run away...

SANDRA (*Murmurs*): Good-bye?... (*A shadow over her*)

ALFREDO (*Lighted*): And I say: Stay... (*A shadow over him*) And you say...

SANDRA (*Lighted, looking into space*): Good-bye... (*A shadow on her*)

ALFREDO (*Lighted*): Sandra!... (*Shadow on him*)

SANDRA (*Lighted, looking into space*): Good-bye! (*Shadow on her*)

ALFREDO (*Lighted*): Don't go! (*Shadow on him. The music dies away. The light slowly returns to normal as HE continues speaking.*) And I look for you... And you've gone away... forever. (*SHE watches him intently.*) And I wake up frightened... because that window doesn't open and you have gone. Sandra, child, all of us here... And René, too. Would you like that? (*SANDRA is looking at him, moved. With hard eyes and repressing his indignation, RENÉ appears in the doorway and observes them for a second. The music has stopped.*)

RENÉ: Good evening. (*Father and daughter look at him and regain their composure.*)

ALFREDO (*Still shaky, but warmly*): Hello, my boy! I'll leave you. I'll leave the two of you so that you can work.

RENÉ: Wait, sir. (*Steps forward*) I would like to speak with you.

ALFREDO: With pleasure, René! Won't you sit down? (*Indicates the sofa to him.*)

RENÉ (*Without sitting down*): Sandra, would you mind leaving us alone?

SANDRA: It's surely nothing I can't hear.

RENÉ: Please, leave me alone with your father.

ALFREDO (*Affably*): You intrigue me. But Sandra must stay. Anything you want to tell me she can hear.

SANDRA (*Resolved*): And I am staying.

ALFREDO: So, what can I do for you? But do have a seat, please! (*HE sits. SANDRA remains standing, very attentive.*)

RENÉ (*As he sits down slowly.*): I'm sorry, Sandra.

SANDRA (*Smiling*): You're going to tell me anyhow!

RENÉ (*To ALFREDO*): You wanted it this way! Sandra, I've just had a talk with your brother. He made me a proposition (*To ALFREDO*) of which you are no doubt aware.

SANDRA: What kind of proposition?

RENÉ: Why don't you explain it yourself, sir? You must have approved it.

ALFREDO (*Cautious*): It depends on what he said to you.

SANDRA: What did he say?

RENÉ: He offered me 400,000 dollars if I leave Spain for good.

SANDRA (*Appalled*): What are you saying?

RENÉ: According to him, a donation to my country. Without documentation, because it would really be for me! I suppose you see the point.

SANDRA: Did you know that, Papa?

RENÉ (*Caustic*): How could he not know it? (*HE gets up angrily.*)

SANDRA (*To her father*): You knew about it!

ALFREDO (*Gets up*): Yes.

SANDRA: And you approved it!

ALFREDO: No.

RENÉ: (*Confronting him*): No? (*HE goes closer to him threateningly.*) Then, why did you let him do it? (*ALFREDO steps back.*)

ALFREDO (*to SANDRA*): I let him do it, reluctantly, to see what this young man of yours was made of. And I told Javi that my plan was very different and that it was going to surprise him. And you already know what it is...

RENÉ (*Controlling himself*): I will limit myself to saying one thing to you, sir: I came to tell you to your face that I've flatly rejected that repugnant bribe!

SANDRA (*Putting two and two together*): Was it Javi you were talking to on the phone just a while ago?

ALFREDO: Yes. (*LORENZA enters unexpectedly with the tea service on a tray. An uncomfortable silence. LORENZA leaves the tray on the table.*) We didn't call you, Mommy!

LORENZA: If I'd waited any longer, you'd have to drink it cold. I'll leave it there. (*Murmurs as SHE exits*) Big shot! (*Leaves mumbling*)

ALFREDO: I have to admit I appreciate her. Sometimes she manages to calm our nerves.

RENÉ: Not mine! But there's nothing more to say. If you want me to leave Spain, you'll have to resort to other means. Shall we go, Sandra?

SANDRA (*Indecisive*): Yes... let's...

ALFREDO: No, please!

RENÉ (*Shouts*): Come on, Sandra!

ALFREDO (*Runs to place himself between them and the door*): Not before you hear me out! (*Angry, RENÉ tries to push him aside.*)

SANDRA: René, no!

ALFREDO (*Strongly*): I don't want you to leave Spain and Sandra knows it. (*Turns his back on RENÉ, looks out at the door and closes it carefully*) And I can tell you that you've passed the test brilliantly.

RENÉ: I don't have any faith in your test. Or in you either! And Sandra would do well to doubt you too.

ALFREDO: My daughter knows I'm speaking the truth. (*Unsure, SANDRA looks at her father and goes and sits in one to the side chairs.*)

RENÉ: Does she? Look at her! You came back to this place to keep an eye on her and separate us. (*Laughs*) You can put your mind at ease! We're not going to get married. (*SANDRA looks at him crestfallen.*) And her wealth won't end up in my hands. But I'll stay at Sandra's side as long as she wishes it!

ALFREDO: That's the uncertain part. Will you stay? Or will you leave one day after you've had all you want from her?

SANDRA: Papa!

ALFREDO: Come now, children! Do you think I'm a fool? You weren't going to be an exception to the rule in these times of do as you please. And I know how to be tolerant... Besides, I don't have any other choice.

SANDRA: Papa, don't say anymore!

ALFREDO (*Affably*): Are you going to be the modest one now?

RENÉ (*Somberly*): Let's go, Sandra.

ALFREDO (*Gravely*): René, she loves you. (*SANDRA is about to speak and he raises his voice.*) She loves you as she's never loved anyone else! (*To SANDRA*) I know it for a fact, dear. I'm perfectly informed.

SANDRA (*Annoyed*): Oh!

ALFREDO (*To RENÉ*): And I think she'll never stop loving you, because she's my own child and I know her well! (*He has gone close to him and gently pushes him back.*) And I don't want her to suffer if you decide to end your relationship. (*Near the side chairs*) Sit down and listen. Both of you listen. (*He presses his shoulder.*) Sit down! (*RENÉ does so reluctantly.*) I prefer that you not go, not even from this house, where I know you've slept often. Listen to my real proposition, which has nothing to do with those dollars my son is offering you to break up with Sandra. You listen too, my dearest. (*HE steps away from them and paces.*) For some time I've been thinking about creating a great cultural foundation.

RENÉ: Why not? It's a custom with potentates!

ALFREDO (*Smiles*): Do you mean that I'd create it to cleanse my image of earlier questionable activities?

RENÉ: And to avoid taxes.

ALFREDO: I don't mind pleading guilty on both counts. And why not? If this world is hopelessly imperfect, let's at least let money generate culture. (*HE goes closer to RENÉ.*) René, you have talent and you proved yourself to be a decent man. You could very well be the head of that foundation. With my daughter. The two of you directing it as friends, or as husband and wife, if you prefer that. (*RENÉ is astounded; SANDRA, surprised. Brief pause.*) Your lives would be dedicated to the noblest undertakings and you could realize together, your dearest dreams...

SANDRA (*With initial hope*): René...

RENÉ: And if I have to return to my country?

ALFREDO: Why should you, if you haven't up to now? And let me say this: I don't see any future for you in your country. And I'm not criticizing you for not having returned; on the contrary, I applaud it. We all have the right to live as best we can in this hard world. You help your own people and you do the right thing, but you could help them even more if you stayed here as head of my foundation. Scholarships for students, publications, technical collaboration. I would approve of that. It's not a reactionary foundation that I want to create.

RENÉ (*Coldly*): Would you really give your approval? I doubt very much, when the time came, that you'd permit all I'd want to do.

ALFREDO: Get those prejudices out of your head and understand once and for all! The autonomy of both of you in making decisions would be very ample and it would be stipulated in your contracts. And as for Sandra... Do you still believe in that old dictum about rich girls only being allowed to marry, or pair off with, well-heeled young men of family? (*Paces. A fleeting glance toward the window*) Thousands of rich men have married poor girls...

RENÉ: Because of society's subordination of women to men.

ALFREDO: More clichés? There are also poor men who marry rich women.

RENÉ: It amounts to the same thing. It's the power of money that speaks.

ALFREDO (*Laughs*): Well, for the scrupulous ones like you, there also exists the separation of property in marriage.

RENÉ: You want to put me into your world, and it's the same world as your son's!

ALFREDO: And yours! Since you've studied in it, and you live... And love in it. Fine. Are we all calmer? Then let's talk more about it.

SANDRA (*Timidly*): René... we could do such beautiful and useful things... Don't you think?

RENÉ (*Looks down*): Sandra, we have to talk.

SANDRA: Papa is sincere, and he likes you...

ALFREDO: And in the popular sense of the word, I am not political. I have no prejudices against what is being attempted in your land; I only think... that experiment is not viable... and that ultimately you'll find more reasonable solutions. There must be on this unfortunate planet. (*RENÉ shakes his head, frowning.*) Sure, I know you're reluctant to accept it. But do recognize that, as they say, I'm putting it all on the table.

RENÉ (*On edge*): What are you trying to achieve with that incredible fairy tale offer? Why are you doing it?

ALFREDO (*Gravely*): For Sandra's happiness. (*Jovially*) And for mine! You'll understand that any day now. (*Expansive, he has gone over to the television monitor and turns it slightly toward them.*) Certainly I'd like to hear more of your comments about this little plaything...

RENÉ: Don't you want my answer to your proposition?

SANDRA: Not yet, René!

ALFREDO: No. Not yet. You must think it over. I have no other proposition. While you're thinking it over, why don't you draw up an organizational plan for my foundation?

RENÉ (*Disconcerted*): What?

ALFREDO: It's a job, with proper remuneration, which doesn't bind you to be a part of anything. Will you do it for me?

RENÉ (*Dryly*): I'll have to think that over too.

SANDRA: Yes, René! You could do it better than anyone!

ALFREDO (*With finality*): Meanwhile, let's amuse ourselves a bit. (*HE puts his cassette in the VCR and turns it on. The light begins to dim; the livid glare of the screen is reflected on their faces. A few seconds pass. Struggling against himself. RENÉ gradually turns toward the screen and faced with ALFREDO's silent invitation, ends up sitting in one of the side chairs.*)

SANDRA (*In a low voice*): Now it's passing more rapidly...

ALFREDO: Like life. Age fifteen, sixteen... twenty... (*Light knocks on the door*) What now! (*Turns off the VCR. The light returns to normal. The knocks are repeated.*) Come in! (*The door opens. LORENZA enters, looks at them, and starts toward the table.*) What do you want, Mommy?

LORENZA: To take away the tea service.

ALFREDO (*A bit impatient but with a smile*):   And sniff out what we're cooking up in here. Right?

LORENZA: Sometimes I don't know why I keep on putting up with you.

ALFREDO (*Laughing*):   Well, it's what you've been doing for a long time now.

LORENZA: You can say that again. So, jódese y baile! [Fuck off!] (*Surprise on seeing the tray*) Why, you haven't touched it! Do you want me to warm it up?

ALFREDO: No, thanks. It's getting late. Close the door when you leave.

LORENZA: I can't with the tray in my hands. Close it yourself. (*SHE crosses with the tray. ALFREDO folds his arms and shakes his head in reaction to her insolence.*)

SANDRA (*Getting up*):   I'll do it, Mommy. (*Goes to the door and lets LORENZA pass through.*)

LORENZA (*As SHE walks past her, lowering her voice*):   Keep you eyes open, dear.

ALFREDO: What are you whispering about now?

LORENZA: Nada... Papanatas! [Nothing... You ninny!] (*Exits and SANDRA closes the door.*)

ALFREDO: Papanatas? At least I don't understand what she's saying.

SANDRA: It's best you don't. Weren't you going out, Papa?

ALFREDO: This interests me more. You want to be alone with René, don't you? You can talk with him later. Pay attention to this. (*HE uses the remote.*)

SANDRA: It's not moving now.

ALFREDO: Age twenty-two. Let me remember those years a little more. (*HE positions himself behind them. The room is submerged in the strange penumbra of memory. Very faintly, the Fantasia Impromptu, Opus. 66, of Chopin is heard. ALFREDO turns to look out and confirms that the window across the way remains closed. The three watch the video. Then, silently, the upstage window opens and reveals the enchanting neighbor girl who is sewing in the past. Without turning around, ALFREDO speaks in a low voice.*) You said that this rapid portrait was like an unexpected mirror.

SANDRA (*Lowering her voice in turn*):   At this moment, a motionless mirror.

RENÉ (*Although lowering his voice, still hostile*):   Because, in order to have control over his life, he stops it sometimes.

ALFREDO: Go on!

RENÉ: To go forward like a conqueror one must dream of what could be and perhaps wasn't. He has stopped it when he was twenty, the age when he is looking for something perhaps forgotten. (*Father and daughter look at each other.*) Something that torments him more than other things. Maybe he wants to stop time to catch that forgotten enigma of surprise. As if he opened a window on the enigma. (*Father and daughter look at each other again. A brief pause. RENÉ's tone changes and he becomes calmer as the video captures his interest.*) To stop for a moment is to make it infinite... to try to make it reveal the infinity it encompasses... it would be the definitive insight. (*To ALFREDO*) About you and everything. It's hidden in each second because all of time is in any instant. Yes. In those tiny openings we seek revelations that were denied to us. You doubt that my country will move forward. I doubt that this mirror will reveal your true face. (*To himself, as SANDRA watches him intently*) But, if you want it to answer..., to answer us all..., we'll have to be as motionless as it is now... and very, very silent... (*The three have become frozen. Not even an eye blinks. They remain this way a few seconds under the sounds of the soft music, while the neighbor girl sews in her window outside of time and ALFREDO, with his head half turned again, listens.*)

CURTAIN or FADE OUT

PART TWO

The window of the sitting room is partly open. The door at right is closed. The graph in the left corner has disappeared, leaving in view the large window filled with greenery. On the table a small lamp, two glasses and two small bottles, in addition to the telephone. Everything on that side suggests a different place, which is now completely dark. In the room and in the courtyard, twilight. (*ALFREDO and JAVIER are seated in the side chairs. On the side table by the sofa, JAVIER's portfolios. Faintly the last measures of the final minuet from Bach's First Brandenburg Concerto are heard coming from outside.*)

JAVIER (*Reluctantly*): The plan he's drawn up is excellent.

ALFREDO: I told you so. René has real talent.

JAVIER: But his approach isn't exactly ours. And my sister had a hand in it too.

ALFREDO: Don't put down his merits. It's clear that the best ideas are his. (*A furtive glance upstage. Pleasure on his face because of what he hears from the courtyard.*)

JAVIER: We'll add our own touches. Have you paid the latino yet?

ALFREDO: Not yet. And he's not exactly a latino.

JAVIER: (*Picks up the booklet and goes over the final pages.*) His budget estimates aren't bad.

ALFREDO: I gave him an idea of the annual sum total, and, naturally, the fixed capitalization.

JAVIER: It could turn out to be a major enterprise. But I wonder if it won't be another game that will take you farther away from our affairs.

ALFREDO: On the contrary! It will supplement them.

JAVIER (*Throws the booklet on the table.*): Will it also supplement your videos?

ALFREDO (*Accenting his smile*): You may not believe it, but it will. You'll see.

JAVIER: You never show those tapes... What's their purpose?

ALFREDO: They're... like exercises... one particular exercise.

JAVIER: I don't understand. (*ALFREDO gets up and puts his hand on the VCR.*)

ALFREDO: Like a mirror, an image...

JAVIER: Of what?

ALFREDO: Let's leave it for now. These things don't interest you.

JAVIER: You're right. They don't interest me. Go ahead and amuse yourself. (*HE gets up and walks about. Stops and looks at him.*) Maybe you should see a doctor and get a prescription for an antidepressant.

ALFREDO: I'm not depressed.

JAVIER (*Hesitates before speaking*): We all are at one time or another... I also need to take something to give me a lift at times. Something... maybe you ought to try. If you know how to take it in moderation; it's very effective. A lot of people use it these days...

ALFREDO (*Interrupts him dryly*): Now I'm the one who doesn't understand you.

JAVIER (*After a moment, looking away*): Well, there are things that don't interest you either. But do return to the country place, to your office, to your travels. And give up these playthings once and for all. You seem like a little child!

ALFREDO: Would that I were.

JAVIER (*Repressing his irritation*): Papa, all this is a lot of foolishness.

ALFREDO: That you will respect!

JAVIER: You can't say I don't respect it. But neither you nor Sandra are safe enough in this house.

ALFREDO: We are protected the best ways possible... and what is to happen... nobody can avoid it, not in the city and not out in the country.

JAVIER: What are you saying? Are you starting to believe in all that nonsense about fate? That's for old dramatists. What I fear is god damn chance, which will give us the worst kind of blow if we don't foresee it in time. Don't tempt chance. You're an organizer, you know how to control events and yourself. Keep on controlling and do what suits you best... not some crazy fancy!

ALFREDO: I assure you it suits me to be here.

JAVIER (*Fed up*): Have it your way! Then the offices of the foundation are to be in our palatial headquarters on the Castellana?

ALFREDO: Don't you like the idea? It's the right place for it.

JAVIER: Yes... still... (*Bothered*) Couldn't you close the window? I can't think for that damn music.

ALFREDO: I find it rather agreeable...

JAVIER: At some other time. I was going to say... (*The minuet ends.*) She couldn't have heard us.

ALFREDO: Yes. What were you going to say?

JAVIER: Well, it doesn't matter. (*HE paces.*) Yes, it does! What doesn't seem right to me is your wanting to entrust the foundation to the latino, while you amuse yourself here! What if you pay him for the plans and he takes off?

ALFREDO: To his country?

JAVIER: Wherever!

ALFREDO: You've already seen that he's not going back there and he's not going to leave Sandra.

JAVIER (*Stops*): Or rather, they'll surprise us with a wedding!

ALFREDO: Maybe. And what if they do? (*Goes downstage*) The boy has some fine qualities, and she loves him...

JAVIER: And you can stand there and say that so calmly? We have to prevent that calamity!

ALFREDO: Be careful what you do. If you separate them against their will, she'll love him even more. (*Goes upstage*) Can I fix you something?

JAVIER: No thanks. (*ALFREDO looks toward the courtyard, closes the window and pours a drink for himself.*) Don't you think you should start letting it be known that you're creating your foundation? The news could serve as a good countereffect.

ALFREDO (*Crosses to him with glass in hand*): We'll have to release it, yes... (*Drinks*) Our attorney is moving. He assures me we'll come out of this completely cleared.

JAVIER: But, as president of your bank, they've subpoenaed me to testify.

ALFREDO: You don't say! You were keeping the worst news for last.

JAVIER: You can relax. They're going to think twice before they start legal action against the co-owners of a weapons firm like ours. At most they'll impose a fine on us for having made an unwise investment in good faith.

ALFREDO: We shouldn't have got involved in the first place! (*Drinks, irritated.*)

JAVIER (*Shrugging*): You signed for it yourself!

ALFREDO: You didn't tell me where the funds might end up!

JAVIER: Because you already knew.

ALFREDO: I did not know!

JAVIER (*With a nasty smile*): Have you really forgotten that? Are we going to have to think about having you declared incompetent?

ALFREDO (*Goes toward him angrily*): What did you say? (*THEY look at each other fixedly. ALFREDO takes another step toward his son.*) How long have you been thinking about that?

JAVIER: They were only words I said because I was irritated with you. I've never thought of anything so stupid.

ALFREDO: Now you have! (*Light knocks on the door. They exchange looks. The door opens. SANDRA and RENÉ enter. ALFREDO immediately puts on a pleasant smile. JAVIER, also smiling, turns around toward them.*) Forgive us for having invaded your sanctuary. We're about to leave.

SANDRA: Hello, Papa. (*SHE kisses him and ignores her brother. SHE sits down.*)

RENÉ: Good evening.

JAVIER: Good evening.

ALFREDO: Sit down, René! (*To his daughter*) We were just talking about your magnificent organizational plan for the foundation. (*To RENÉ*) You will, naturally, receive your remuneration for this work.

RENÉ (*Sitting down*): It's not necessary. I don't want any payment for it.

ALFREDO (*Sits down*): Why not? Although you're going to be a part of the leadership, this first contribution should not go unrewarded. We always pay for what we commission.

RENÉ: But Sandra worked with me...

JAVIER: It's different. Don't forget that she actually belongs to the commissioning group rather than the commissioned. Right, little sister? (*SANDRA looks at him coldly and then looks away.*) Hey, I'm here! You haven't even said hello to me...

SANDRA: You and I have nothing to talk about.

JAVIER: How's that? What's with you?

SANDRA (*Gets up and goes to sit beside René*): What you proposed to René is vile.

ALFREDO: Sandra, please!

JAVIER (*Looks at his watch and decides to sit down*): Neither of you should take offence at that. (*To SANDRA*) And you should understand my concern for you. But since René prefers to stay... only a minute ago I was praising the good points of your plan to Papa.

ALFREDO: Sandra, since René is going to work with us, you should put an end to that little disagreement with your brother. Don't you think? (*RENÉ, who was smiling, begins to laugh softly.*)

JAVIER: Do you find it amusing?

RENÉ (*Gets up*): I'm sorry. Please excuse me, all of you. (*As HE crosses to the bar*) May I, sir, fix myself a drink too?

ALFREDO (*With a gesture toward the bar*): For heaven's sake, yes! You must forgive me for not offering. Something for you, Sandra?

SANDRA (*Who watches René closely*): No.

RENÉ (*As HE serves himself*): I was laughing because I couldn't help remembering certain interrogations.

ALFREDO: What interrogations?

RENÉ (*Smiling*): I'm sorry... it's an unfortunate comparison.

JAVIER: Comparison with what?

RENÉ: Please, don't be annoyed... (*Takes a sip*) But I was remembering a certain technique... they applied to me once in my student days. (*A slight laugh*) First comes the tough one, the implacable one. And if he doesn't get anything out of you, another one comes and attempts to soften up the prisoner with some good words and a cigarette.(*An uncomfortable silence.*)

ALFREDO: To be sure, an unfortunate comparison. Because if I'm the second policeman, I haven't asked you to leave but to stay.

RENÉ: Of course, excuse me. I was only thinking that both of you are, in essence, trying for the same result.

ALFREDO: Exactly. Both of us want you to stay. Javier is more forceful about it.

RENÉ: Sorry.

ALFREDO (*Gets up*): Well, then. (*Goes and picks up the booklet*) There's nothing left but getting on with the job with enthusiasm! In your plan...

RENÉ: Again you must excuse me. (*A quick glance at SANDRA.*) I still haven't decided whether I'll be a part of that foundation or not.

SANDRA (*Surprised and worried*): René! Only yesterday you told me...

RENÉ: Yes, we were dreaming together. But I still have to think about it. (*HE has said this with some confusion. There is another uncomfortable silence.*)

JAVIER (*Very softly*): What is it you have to think about? (*SANDRA gets up, her face betraying her disapproval, crosses and sits down in one of the side chairs so that they cannot see her changed appearance.*)

RENÉ (*Looks at the two men and, finally, at SANDRA*): I have to think... about my country. (*Without turning her head, SANDRA gets up, looking terribly upset.*)

JAVIER (*Gets up, now hostile and superior*): Perfect. That means you're still considering my first offer. (*SANDRA turns and looks at him with an expression of distress. JAVIER consults his watch again and picks up his portfolios.*) As far as I'm concerned, that offer still stands... And I suppose with my father's approval. I've let time slip up on me. I'll be seeing you. (*Rapidly, and without looking at anyone, HE exits.*)

ALFREDO (*Weakly*): Yes, to be sure. I was going to say that in this plan...

SANDRA (*Curtly*): Papa, let's not talk about that. (*SHE is observing RENÉ closely. HE puts down his glass, crosses to her and puts his hand on her shoulder.*)

RENÉ: Listen, Sandra... (*SHE rejects his touch.*)

ALFREDO: I'll leave you if you wish...

SANDRA: (*To RENÉ*): Not here. Let's go.

ALFREDO: You can close the door and no one will bother you... (*HE leaves the booklet on the table and takes a few steps.*)

SANDRA (*To her father*): Don't leave. We're going to my apartment.

RENÉ: Maybe we should go to some other place... (*LORENZA appears at the door.*)

SANDRA (*With a bitter smile*): To our eternal afternoon?

RENÉ: No, Sandra. To some café.

SANDRA: To our eternal afternoon or to a nowhere place.

ALFREDO: Your eternal afternoon? What is that?

SANDRA: A joke. A silly thing between us.

LORENZA: Excuse me. Would you like something?

SANDRA: No, Mommy. We're leaving.

LORENZA (*To ALFREDO*): Nothing for you either?

ALFREDO (*His mind on the couple*): Yes... fill my glass again. (*LORENZA takes the glass and goes to the bar.*)

SANDRA (*With a tone of finality, to RENÉ*): Are we going?

RENÉ: Whenever you wish. (*THEY start their exit.*)

ALFREDO: I insist, Sandra. Don't go. You can go with him to your room. It doesn't matter to me. (*LORENZA looks at him with an indefinable expression and goes about her task.*)

SANDRA: No. Good-bye.

ALFREDO (*With a humble smile*): I'd prefer "see you later"...

SANDRA (*Stopping*): I'm afraid that sooner or later it will be "good-bye" for us, Papa.

ALFREDO: I hope that both of you will consider calmly just how marvelous it would be to work together in my foundation... Good-bye for now, Sandra.

SANDRA: Let's go, René. (*SHE exits first and, after a slight bow to ALFREDO, RENÉ exits in turn. A few seconds pass.*)

LORENZA (*Handing the drink to her "master"*): Your glass.

ALFREDO (*Taking the glass mechanically.*): Is my guard outside in the hall?

LORENZA: As always. And the gorilla that follows the girl is down on the street. You can relax. (*ALFREDO swallows his drink. LORENZA glances out the window.*) It's already getting dark. I'm going to my room. (*Starts to go.*)

ALFREDO (*Thinking*): Open the window a little, Mommy. It's getting warm.

LORENZA (*With an ironic grunt, SHE obeys.*): And when it gets warm, all the windows will start opening.

ALFREDO (*Gives her a look*): Of course!

LORENZA: Of course. (*Starts to cross.*)

ALFREDO: Why don't you fix something for yourself and we can talk?

LORENZA (*Surprised*): About what?

ALFREDO: About the happy couple... About things...

LORENZA: There's something I have to do.

ALFREDO: Come on, drink something, and chat with me.

LORENZA (*Sullenly, to herself*): Like we used to.

ALFREDO: What did you say?

LORENZA: Nothing.

ALFREDO: Can I fix you a drink? What would you like?

LORENZA (*Coldly*): If you insist... You've got us trained never to say no to anything. (*SHE goes to the bar.*) I'll do it myself. A little anise won't hurt me.

ALFREDO (*Goes and sits in one of the side chairs.*): Don't look so grim, woman... It's as if all of you were against me.

LORENZA: The things you say. (*Takes a glass from the bar and, after giving it a moment's thought, fills it to the brim. ALFREDO drinks a little.*)

ALFREDO: Do you have a problem with me?

LORENZA: Now that's a question. (*SHE goes closer to him with glass in hand and remains standing.*)

ALFREDO (*Laughing*): Not like that, Mommy... Sit down here. (*HE indicates the other chair.*)

LORENZA: At your command. (*Sits*)

ALFREDO: Drink, drink a little. (*First SHE takes a tiny sip and immediately takes pleasure in a rather large swallow.*) Not so fast! You'll make yourself tipsy.

LORENZA: What difference does it make?

ALFREDO: You look like you've been to a funeral! Cheer up, Mommy! There are always problems, but I think they're going to be resolved and we'll all be together right here. Including them. And then you'll stay too, won't you?

LORENZA: I'll always be where my girl is. You already know that.

ALFREDO: By the way, have you arranged for that dressmaker to come by and speak with Sandra?

LORENZA: Sandra said to wait until we went to the other apartment.
ALFREDO: And if you don't go? René is stubborn, but I think they'll end up deciding to stay here. Why don't you speak with Sandra and call the dressmaker? It'll be all the more reason for Sandra to be here. Do you see my point?
LORENZA: Don't worry. If Sandra stays, I'll call that stupid woman.
ALFREDO (*Surprised*) Stupid? How do you know she's stupid? Have you talked with her?
LORENZA: No.
ALFREDO: Then don't judge her by what others have said.
LORENZA: No one has said anything to me. It's my own opinion. (*Takes another sip*) Uf! This is very strong. (*Leaves the glass on the end table.*)
ALFREDO: So it's your own opinion, is it? And just how did you come to that conclusion?
LORENZA: You're right. I don't know anything about her.
ALFREDO: Of course not! She couldn't be stupid. Withdrawn, unsociable, if you like. But with excellent tastes, to judge by the music she plays. You'll see if she comes here. You'll probably find that you are a lot alike.
LORENZA: Qué? [What?]
ALFREDO: Maybe she's like you, and you aren't the least bit stupid. (*Laughs*) You might even become friends.
LORENZA: No! (*The light in the courtyard is fading.*)
ALFREDO: Why not? If she's going to work for our Sandra, she may be coming frequently.
LORENZA: Don't get your hopes up. (*SHE takes her glass and drains it.*)
ALFREDO: Hopes for what? It was you yourself who suggested she come!
LORENZA: Yes. So that you could see what she was like.
ALFREDO: I? Mommy, the anise is making you talk nonsense. You say that she is stupid, that I'm hoping for something. I don't know what you're talking about.
LORENZA: Farsante! [You fraud!]
ALFREDO: Fraud? Is that what you called me?
LORENZA: How do I know? I don't translate.
ALFREDO (*Gets up*): With only one little glass... I thought you were a better drinker.
LORENZA: It's not the anise. It's because we've known each other for many years.
ALFREDO (*Paces*): Since I was a boy. But then you were nicer to all of us. Now you've become rather cross. Especially since I came back here.

LORENZA: Long before that. (*SHE leaves her glass on the side table.*)

ALFREDO: All right. Long before.

LORENZA: When you raped me. No; a bit later.

ALFREDO (*Jolted*): Lorenza!

LORENZA: I'm called by my name now? It wasn't that way then. Then I was the accommodating nanny. Because I was a bit older than you but still just a girl.

ALFREDO: We had agreed to never speak of that again.

LORENZA: I've kept my mouth shut.

ALFREDO (*Contrite*): I was only a boy full of desire... And when I came to you, you consented.

LORENZA: Like a caring nanny, according to you. Because you already had your eye on the neighbor's girl.

ALFREDO: I liked to watch her... And I liked you too. I loved you.

LORENZA: And you told me so often... while you were watching the neighbor girl across the way. Afterwards you married another fool, and you always had your mistresses even before she died. Engañoso [Two-timer].

ALFREDO: What did you say?

LORENZA: You talk out of both sides of your mouth and get away with it. And I, the real mommy ever since your daughter was born. Years and years, up to this very day. Bless her.

ALFREDO: You chose to do that of your own free will, Mommy. All of it; what was between us and the dedication to Sandra. And I've always been grateful for that.

LORENZA: Oh, yes! You've even given me money for my old age. You always made a show of paying well.

ALFREDO: It wasn't a payment!

LORENZA: Call it what you will. (*Short silence*)

ALFREDO (*Sadly*): Lorenza, you should have married.

LORENZA: I never even tried. In those times there were a lot of obstacles to second-hand marriages.

ALFREDO (*With a sad and troubled laugh*): Lorenza, I can't believe it. Is it possible you're jealous?

LORENZA: Don't talk nonsense. (*But SHE avoids eye contact.*)

ALFREDO (*HE leaves his glass on the table and goes over to put his hands on her shoulder.*): If you're not, why not remember that as something beautiful and good that happened to us and let's keep on getting along together? You've never been a servant but a good and trusted friend. A member of the family.

LORENZA: Really? You call me Lorenza but I can't say your name.

ALFREDO: It's only a social custom... (*HE sits beside her again. In the courtyard nocturnal shadow reigns.*)

LORENZA: That's it. Social custom. Like rich boys getting in the beds of servant girls. (*Angry, SHE gets up and walks away from ALFREDO.*) Another old custom!

ALFREDO: You let me! Maybe out of pity, and I'll always be grateful to you. But... didn't you feel something more than pity for me?... (*Behind the curtains of the facing window, a light comes on. LORENZA doesn't fail to notice and SHE starts to go toward ALFREDO with noticeable emotion, perhaps on the verge of tears, as HE watches the window fixedly. SHE starts to speak and closes her mouth, stifling with effort an insult. Annoyed, ALFREDO utters:*) What were you going to say to me? Some foreign slang?

LORENZA: Not this time. (*SHE picks up the glasses.*)

ALFREDO (*Looking down*): You don't understand. Do me a favor and let me be alone.

LORENZA: No favor of mine. You already left me alone years ago. But now I'm glad. (*SHE exits rapidly at right with the glasses in hand as ALFREDO gets up and takes a few steps toward her.*)

ALFREDO: Lorenza! You let me do it! (*Stops and murmurs to himself.*) You let me... (*HE turns upstage and goes toward the window. HE observes the other window and looks again toward the door, as if making a confused comparison. HE looks again intently at the window across the courtyard. The light fades rapidly until only the curtains of ISOLINA SANCHEZ remain lit. Finally the light behind the curtains is extinguished too, as the light comes up on the left side. In the window the cool gleam of thick greenery. The small lamp comes on and the downstage area is lit by amber lights from the side. With an arm around each other, SANDRA and RENÉ enter right.*)

RENÉ: Why were you so set on coming here?

SANDRA: It's a good place to talk in peace.

RENÉ: With a thug in the bar downstairs. And maybe another one outside on the street. (*HE goes to the little table and begins to fill two glasses.*)

SANDRA (*With a little laugh*): We lost them.

RENÉ (*Takes a sip*): I don't think so.

SANDRA: Well, if they're downstairs, let them wait. They're not going to come up. (*SHE goes closer to him; tenderly.*) And this is our private terrain... Remember. (*takes the other glass*) This is where we made love for the first time. (*Drinks*)

RENÉ (*Serious*): But today we've only come to talk.

SANDRA (*Puts down her glass and throws her arms around his neck*): Aren't you going to let me seduce you? (*SHE kisses him over and over.*)

RENÉ (*Responding to her kisses*): Dearest, listen to me...

SANDRA: Yes, but later! Do you know what it's been like not having you for two months?

RENÉ (*As THEY continue to caress each other*): And for me... (*SHE leads him to the sofa, where they fall together.*)

SANDRA: My René... my René...

RENÉ (*HE manages to pull away gently.*): Please, Sandra. There is so much to say... And it's already night...

SANDRA: Night. Look at the lights on the plants.

RENÉ: It's artificial.

SANDRA: Not for us. Here we're in our eternal afternoon.

RENÉ: You said yourself that it sounded silly.

SANDRA: Not in this place. Do you remember? There's no day or night. We both said it right here. There's only love... love. (*HE kisses her again but tries to move her away from him gently.*)

RENÉ: Sandra, I don't have a right to your love if you don't listen to me first.

SANDRA (*Annoyed, SHE moves away and picks up her glass.*): Alright. Didn't you want to talk? Then talk. (*Drinks*)

RENÉ: Don't make it difficult for me... Let's try to understand each other as much as we can.

SANDRA: What's there to understand, if we love each other? We'll direct the foundation and we'll continue to be happy. Isn't it marvelous?

RENÉ: Sandra... You still aren't mine. You still belong to your world, which isn't my world. Your father's offer won you over at once, but I must give it more thought. Because I'm not cut out to be just another rich business executive.

SANDRA: Why not? My father couldn't have put it more plainly. You'll be an executive who can give a lot of assistance to your country...

RENÉ: Until your father, and your brother, and your bank say no. And I'll already be trapped.

SANDRA: Don't you trust my father?

RENÉ: We've talked about that many times. He's trapped too.

SANDRA: But with all his faults, he's a man of his word.

RENÉ: Sandra, it's not a question of personal qualities. Your father may be a good person, but he's tied to his interests. And that foundation will have to serve them too.

SANDRA: But we will do something...

RENÉ: And that's the reason for my doubts.

SANDRA (*Lovingly*): Stop doubting.

RENÉ: I have to have doubts. You still don't know how sinister your world can become... Have you heard of Mundifisa?

SANDRA: I don't know... What is it?

RENÉ: An investment and financing corporation. Maybe they've put some of your own money into it for you.

SANDRA: The bank administers it, but they don't move anything without consulting me. I don't remember ever hearing that name.

RENÉ: Well, if they do propose it to you one day, be warned. A Colombian friend of mine had a job in it, and he told me confidentially... But no. I'm sorry. I mustn't talk about it yet. I promised him.

SANDRA: What did we agree? Are you going to talk to me or aren't you?

RENÉ: Yes. But about the foundation. While you and I worked so happily, year after year, (*Ironically*) and I became more and more prosperous... my people would continue struggling, if they hadn't crushed them yet. And maybe then I'd not feel like a... deserter.

SANDRA: A deserter? You're helping your people. And there are also a thousand things to remedy here and assist.

RENÉ: Not like there. Everything is more fixed here, more difficult to change. And it can make our efforts useless.

SANDRA: And don't you suppose there will be corruption in your country... difficult to change?

RENÉ: There is already.

SANDRA: Then?

RENÉ: We can deal with it in time! The people still believe in the future. But they're terribly tired, hungry, and miserable... Some who could make a difference leave and don't return. It's necessary to try to keep their spirits up, so that they'll go on resisting under the endless hounding they can hardly endure. To help them there rather than from outside. It's urgent. Because they're almost overwhelmed.

SANDRA (*Sadly*): You want to go back.

RENÉ: I've been here for years, Sandra. I hardly speak the way they do, I've almost lost my accent... I'm like those who are fleeing my country now, only I fled a long time ago. I have all I need and I have you, who are the greatest happiness of my life. And it suits my government for me to stay in Spain, because all the international aid doesn't amount to much. (*Laughs bitterly*) Now you see what a strange guy I am: I have all I could desire and I think of returning to that hell.

SANDRA: If you want to return, I'll go with you.

RENÉ: Sandra, you don't know...

SANDRA (*Putting her hand on his shoulder and interrupting him.*): I'm also fed up with this life of wealth and lies. If you're a strange guy, I'm like you. Do you think I wouldn't be able to put up with deprivation and danger?

RENÉ: But I don't want you to! I wouldn't be able to look you in the eye knowing I'd condemned you to such a hard life. And maybe even to sorrow.

SANDRA (*Laughs*): How little you know me. I can deal with anything! If something gets in my way, I can shove it aside. (*Laughs again*) I even know a bit of karate. Listen: you go, and a little later I'll leave.

RENÉ: Love, you don't know what it's like. And I wouldn't want them to say that my companion lives better than the others and, incidentally, I do too, because she can buy for me on the black market.

SANDRA: Rot! Others are probably already doing it. Go on, you aren't touching your drink. (*SHE drinks, and HE takes a sip from his glass.*)

RENÉ: I have no right to impose that life on you, Sandra. Over there, even in the capital, there are constant skirmishes, because the mercenaries make incursions from the jungle. And the children have come to believe that war is a normal way of life; they haven't known anything else. It's decreed that they all go to school, but the rest of the day they scavenge what they can to eat. They're on their own! Because their parents are working and the wages don't even cover the bare necessities. Street children from necessity... A pound of meat costs a tenth of a month's pay, so they never have it. In the schools, one book for every ten students. Notebooks and pencils, all rationed and shared. For the adults, any gift is a treasure. A ball point, a watch, not to speak of a bottle of perfume... Visitors return with little more than they're wearing: they've given away their shirts, their pants... In the pharmacies, there are no aspirin or toothpaste; only substitutes that they invent. You won't find a decent bar of soap; they make it with fat and whatever will work... No toilet paper either; they use newspapers. That's why the black market is inevitable. You can get whatever you want on it, but who can afford it? And in dollars? That's for the foreigners who carry them and the embassies... speculation is a disease that's spreading and even the unions oppose the government at times. The powerful of the earth have condemned us all to that with their implacable blockade.

SANDRA: Then... if it's as you say... it's hopeless!

RENÉ: No, not as long as we resist. And it's necessary for me to join that struggle.

SANDRA: René, if I were at your side, I'd find a way to be a part of that struggle too.

RENÉ: My dearest, I'm not crazy and I won't drag you along with me. Over there our love might simply burn out and nothing but ashes would remain.

SANDRA: And if you go, how long would it last? I don't want it to die! Don't go!

RENÉ: Sandra, help me.

SANDRA: To go without me? I can't and I won't! Don't kill our love.

RENÉ: Do you believe I shouldn't go?

SANDRA: I don't know. I only know that if you do go, I'll join you. (*Gently*) And if you don't go, I'll love you here for the rest of my life. (*Laughs nervously*) And let's leave it at that! You decide. (*SHE throws herself into his arms and kisses him several times.*) You!... You!...

RENÉ: Sandra, you're not helping me this way. (*His expression has changed. HE pulls away from her, gets up, and walks toward the proscenium.*)

SANDRA (*Imperiously*): You decide! But if you go, don't count on me not to follow you afterwards.

RENÉ: It's not only that... if I go... it mustn't be with empty hands.

SANDRA (*Suddenly changed, SHE gets up and approaches him.*): Do you want money?

RENÉ (*Turning toward her*): No more of yours! I'm not some gigolo who lives off rich girls. (*Very affected, SHE moves away from him toward centerstage.*)

SANDRA: I wish I didn't understand you... Are you thinking about my brother's offer?

RENÉ: It's my turn to ask you a question: Do I have the right to refuse it when my people are enduring such terrible needs? Yes, I could accept your brother's money. It matters little to me if he thinks I'm going to appropriate it for myself.

SANDRA (*As SHE sorts out her feelings*): Let's do this... Accept it, go home and turn it over. A few months later I'll arrive, and you can no longer return anything... We'll have outwitted him, but that doesn't matter to me either.

RENÉ (*With a sad smile*): Sandra, some people would tell you that that was the authentic revolutionary spirit... But I don't believe it and I'm convinced that it's another of the errors we must correct. We must be people of our word.

SANDRA: Then... I can't believe it!... Are you telling me that you would accept Javier's offer... and that we must not see each other again?

RENÉ (*Weakly*): If I go, yes.

SANDRA: That we should part forever?

RENÉ: If I don't stay, it will have to be that way.

SANDRA (*With curt sarcasm*): Because you are a man of your word.

RENÉ: And because I ought not reject that gift to my country. (*Deeply moved*) Sandra, maybe our eternal afternoon has only been a dream. (*Looks at the window*) Within a few hours the light will go off and the afternoon will disappear from that window. Who knows if some day our devotion will end, even if I didn't go... And that would be even more painful. But I beg you to decide. Should I leave?

SANDRA: Why, if you've already made up your mind?

RENÉ (*Anguished*): No! If you have reasons for me not to go, that I haven't managed to discover... Tell them to me, if you have!

SANDRA: Reasons? If you loved me, you wouldn't hesitate to stay. I'm beginning to understand... that you've never truly loved me.

RENÉ: Don't say that!

SANDRA: But I... I do love you!

RENÉ: And I you! With all my being!

SANDRA (*Tearful*): I offer you everything! Even living in your country! Even more than what my brother has offered you to separate us, and your conscience rejects it! But not Javier's money, because it's quicker and more certain! For that you have a different conscience!

RENÉ (*Going toward her*): It is the same! Don't you understand that?

SANDRA (*Without looking at him*): And he still wants me to be the one to tell him to go, when he's already decided it.

RENÉ (*Taking another step toward her*): No!

SANDRA (*Steps back*): Don't come any closer! (*SHE covers her eyes with her hands to contain and dry her tears.*) How blind I've been! (*Faces him.*) You're giving me up because my brother puts a few million in your pocket.

RENÉ: To hand over to my country! And I still haven't said that I'm going to go. Don't you realize the terrible dilemma your brother has put me in?

SANDRA: To hand over to your country?

RENÉ: It's what I would do. You know that very well.

SANDRA: I don't know anything anymore... suddenly you seem like another person...

RENÉ: Sandra, you offend me! How can you even suspect that I could keep that money for myself? Don't you know me?

SANDRA (*Takes a deep breath and gets control of herself*): To be honest, I don't know you. Since you've already made up your mind, go. And the sooner the better, Good-bye. (*SHE walks to the right.*)

RENÉ (*Right behind her*): I swear to you that my greatest desire is to stay... Let's talk more...

SANDRA (*Stops*): Everything's been said!

RENÉ: Not yet! I'll go with you!

SANDRA: No! (*And SHE exits. RENÉ stops, worried and disheartened.*)

RENÉ (*Mumbles*): It's not possible... It's not possible... (*Slow fade, during which only the greenery of the window glows and then goes out as again we hear, now with impressive force, the movement from Beethoven's Third Symphony. In the dense blackness, a sudden light on RENÉ in the act of searching. His voice and ALFREDO's immediately after, although anguished, are heard as whispers, without the least emphasis.*) Sandra! Sandra! I'll stay! (*Darkness and a sudden light on ALFREDO, in a twisted position in a chair.*)

ALFREDO: Sandra, don't say good-bye to me! (*Darkness and light on RENÉ, on the other side of the stage.*)

RENÉ: Don't go! I'll do what you want! (*Darkness and light on ALFREDO.*)

ALFREDO: We'll be a real family! (*Darkness. Another light on RENÉ in another place.*)

RENÉ: We'll live in our eternal afternoon! (*Darkness. Light on ALFREDO.*)

ALFREDO: Time is in our hands! (*Darkness.*)

SANDRA (*Her voice, distant*): Good-bye... (*Light on RENÉ in another place.*)

RENÉ: Don't run away from me! (*Darkness.*)

SANDRA (*Her voice, very distant*): Good-bye... (*Darkness, in which the solemn sounds of the Eroica Symphony fade away as the two lamps in the sitting room come up. In the courtyard, deep night. ALFREDO, in a short robe, is seated in front of the VCR, which is playing. The business graph has again covered the false greenery of the window in the corner, but is hardly visible in the dense shadow.*)

ALFREDO (*Murmurs*): Don't make me dream my nightmare again... Don't go. (*HE watches his video with an obsessive gaze. LORENZA appears at the door and observes him. She is wearing a robe or housecoat.*)

LORENZA: Aren't you going to bed? (*ALFREDO is startled; he turns off the VCR with the remote and turns toward her.*)

ALFREDO: What?

LORENZA (*Takes a few steps*): It's very late. Go to bed.

ALFREDO (*Looking at his watch*): What time is it?

LORENZA: After four.

ALFREDO: And Sandra hasn't come back.

LORENZA (*With sarcasm*): And that worries you?

ALFREDO: You're not worried?

LORENZA: It's not as if it's the first time. Likely she's gone to her apartment.

ALFREDO: Then why haven't you gone to bed?

LORENZA (*Hesitates and speaks*): Oh, damn it! Because the girl hasn't come home! (*SHE sits down brusquely in a convenient place.*) I always wait for her even if I don't know whether she's going to return.

ALFREDO (*Without looking at her*): So do I. Where do you suppose she is? You don't think something's happened to her? (*Looks at her*) We always think those things, don't we?

LORENZA: Thank heaven they never happen.

ALFREDO: No. And she has a guard. (*Consults his watch.*)

LORENZA: But it is very late.

ALFREDO: She must have gone to her apartment. (*Brief silence.*)

LORENZA (*Starts to get up*): I'm going to bed.

ALFREDO: Mommy, you have indeed been her real mother.

LORENZA (*Stays seated*): Then don't give her another one.

ALFREDO: What are you saying? I don't intend...

LORENZA: Of course you intend to. And it doesn't make me dance with joy. (*ALFREDO observes her out of the corner of his eye as he gets up, leaves the remote on the television set and lights a cigarette. HE paces and smokes. LORENZA begins to get up again.*)

ALFREDO: You don't miss a thing... Yes, I intend to. (*Now standing, SHE fixes her eyes on him. HE speaks with humility.*) Would it be so hard for you to accept it? You and I are old now...

LORENZA: I'm old. Not you. And I don't have Sandra either. Nobody has her.

ALFREDO: Then we're going to get her back together!

LORENZA: With René?

ALFREDO (*Nods*): With René.

LORENZA: With Miss Isolina Sánchez?

ALFREDO (*Steps back a little and speaks gently*):   You've always been understanding, Mommy. Understand me now...

LORENZA: Don't call me Mommy. If I don't bring her, you'll bring that woman. You'll get what you want as always. (*HE moves farther away. SHE goes toward him.*) But don't think that I'm going to be a mommy for her too. Nor for you! For Sandra and for her René, yes... They're young. For you and that woman, no.

ALFREDO (*Takes her by the elbows*): Lorenza, if you loved me little once, don't hold a grudge now. That's over and you can't love me any longer...

LORENZA: No.

ALFREDO: Then for the feeling you once had for me and no longer have, go on seeing me as the boy I was, and tolerate me as then, when we loved each other... Because you did love me a little. Admit it.

LORENZA (*After a long sigh, SHE bows her head.*): I consented because I was afraid.

ALFREDO (*Amazed, HE steps back.*): Of what?

LORENZA: You were very domineering and unpredictable. I was afraid you'd invent some story so that your parents would throw me out, if I didn't give in to you.

ALFREDO: I?

LORENZA (*Turns to look at him*): My father had died in the war. Did you know that?

ALFREDO (*Doubtful*): Yes... I seem to remember...

LORENZA: My mother and I were left with nothing. I was hardly more than a child when I had to look for work, and there wasn't much around. Suddenly a stroke of luck: a chance to come into a house like this one. And I was scared to death that they'd throw me out without even enough to buy food... I've told myself a thousand times that I shouldn't have been afraid... But I was.

ALFREDO: No... I can't believe what you did with me was from fear... Was that the only reason?

LORENZA (*Moves away from him, upset.*): What do I know? (*Tears well up.*) I didn't know everything then... not even how I felt... Plain ignorant. (*Moved, ALFREDO starts toward her and stops when she speaks again.*) And now you return to this house agog again over Isolina Sánchez. (*Her voice shakes.*) What are you after? The same as with me and all the others? Why, she's practically an old woman! You can get better ones for pay. (*Lowers her voice.*) And she won't be able to give you children.

ALFREDO: Lorenza, please!

LORENZA (*With sudden fury*): You're crazy! Crazy between that window and that stupid gadget! (*Points to the VCR.*) To remember, I've heard you say. Ha! You'd remember better if you looked at the photos of your family and friends, like people in their right minds do. But not you! You, looking at yourself over and over to compare the nose you have now with the one you had then... (*SHE brings her face close to his.*) Because what really matters to you is yourself and nobody else. Not that dressmaker. Not even Sandra.

ALFREDO (*Seizes her arm*): Lorenza, that's enough!

LORENZA: Let me go! (*SHE frees herself with a brusque movement.*) I'll say anything I like. You don't tell me what to do any longer. (*SHE turns her back on him and is starting to exit when the ring of the telephone stops her. THEY are both startled. ALFREDO takes a few uncertain steps toward the phone and stops, looking at his watch.*)

ALFREDO: Four-thirty. (*SHE gives a muffled groan.*) Maybe it's... some business matter...

LORENZA (*Quietly*): At this hour? (*The phone keeps on ringing. ALFREDO doesn't dare pick up.*) My God!... (*Then HE does.*)

ALFREDO: Hello... Yes, speaking! Well? (*Listens with growing anxiety.*) What do you mean you lost her? It's your business not to lose her! And you have your car!...

LORENZA (*Twisting her hands, SHE has moved closer.*): Sandra? (*ALFREDO makes a gesture to her to keep quiet.*)

ALFREDO: What? How's that? I don't understand!... Have you found her or not? Well then, thank heaven for that! Where?...

LORENZA: Where?

ALFREDO (*In half voice*): In front of her apartment. (*To the phone*) Then, why are you calling?...

LORENZA (*Very softly*): Oh, my God!...

ALFREDO: What?... (*Excitedly*) What are you saying? I don't understand you at all!... What do you mean on the sidewalk? No! (*HE is shaking visibly.*) But... is she alive? I'm asking you if she's alive!... Answer! (*ALFREDO stifles a terrible moan. The receiver slips out of his hand. At his side, LORENZA strikes him on the chest with her clenched fists.*)

LORENZA: Bastard! Fool! Son of a bitch! (*SHE screams between sobs before Alfredo's frightened eyes, but he does not react. Sudden darkness and simultaneous repetition of the Beethoven motif. Little by little the music loses intensity and the brightness of a radiant morning returns to*

*the room. The window is open wide. The window across the courtyard
remains closed. For a few moments, no one onstage. The music, now
very faint, stops. RENÉ enters and stands looking at the empty room.
He crosses with a pained sigh, glances distractedly toward the courtyard
and goes over to the VCR, considering it with a sad smile. After taking
a look toward the right, he picks up the remote and turns on the VCR.
The video begins. Leaving the picture on, he freezes the tape.
ALFREDO enters right, dressed in mourning, and stops.)*

ALFREDO: Don't touch that! (*RENÉ leaves the remote on the top of the
television monitor. ALFREDO takes a few steps into the room.*) I wasn't
expecting to see you again. Why have you come?

RENÉ: To pick up the things that belong to me.

ALFREDO: Then do it and leave.

RENÉ: I already have. Everything's in my suitcase in the hallway.

ALFREDO: Then what are you doing here?

RENÉ: I was waiting to return the keys. (*Takes them from his pocket, holds
them up for inspection and leaves them on the table.*) I would have given
them to Lorenza, but I haven't seen her. I'd like to say good-bye to her
too.

ALFREDO: Lorenza left days ago.

RENÉ: Where did she go?

ALFREDO: I don't know. Anything else?

RENÉ: No. (*Crosses to leave. Turns around.*) That is, yes. Because at the
cemetery I preferred not to speak to you.

ALFREDO: I noticed that you were afraid to.

RENÉ: It's not that I was afraid. There simply was no moment. But now
I would like to know more about... how it happened. And to confirm my
suspicions.

ALFREDO: Oh, you suspect something? Well, there's something I'd like to
know too. Why did you let her leave that place alone?

RENÉ: We had an argument.

ALFREDO (*Irritated*): An argument! And you let her go.

RENÉ: No! I ran after her but she'd already started her car... You know,
sir, how quick she was. I admit I was slow in thinking where to look for
her. And I spent hours going to places we frequented... When I finally
decided to go to the apartment, the police had already arrived and they'd
taken her away. I only saw the doorman and some bystanders who were
still talking about it on the sidewalk... And I found out that you and your
son had gone too.

ALFREDO: All those who should have watched over her failed. And that includes you! (*Lowers his voice.*) If I have any power at all I'll see that they throw you out of this country.

RENÉ (*Takes out a plane ticket, which HE shows*): No need. I'm returning to mine.

ALFREDO: Too late! If you hadn't known her, I would have regained her... in this house... (*His voice breaks. HE slumps down in one of the side chairs.*) You can't know... What it is to lose... a daughter... what it is... to die for her... Because I... am already dead.

RENÉ: I won't cry in front of you. I only want you to tell me... how it happened.

ALFREDO (*Tries to control his emotions*): You already know.

RENÉ: Not everything.

ALFREDO: And what more do you want to know? She was attacked. Surely they knew who she was... Someone was waiting for her and she resisted... That's how she was, brave and unconcerned about her own safety.

RENÉ: Who attacked her?

ALFREDO: We don't know. But we will. A passerby saw it from a distance. It was some punk. I swear he won't escape.

RENÉ: Why did her attack her?

ALFREDO: How do I know! To kidnap her maybe... to assault her.

RENÉ: No. After he slashed her, he took her money and ran. It's typical.

ALFREDO: Get out of my sight! I can't bear the presence of the guilty.

RENÉ: Neither can I. (*Brief pause*)

ALFREDO: What are you saying?

RENÉ (*Going closer to him*): Whenever you asked her to be careful, you always talked about sexual assaults, of kidnappings... Never of another thing. That made me think.

ALFREDO: Think? Think what?

RENÉ: And I managed to get some information. Relax! It was all very confidential. And although the press says they have to be found, the ones at the top never are. But you're one of them, at least in this country.

ALFREDO (*Averts his eyes*): I don't know what you're talking about.

RENÉ: About Mundifisa, your cartel. (*As if moved by a spring, ALFREDO leaps to his feet and confronts René with eyes flashing anger.*)

ALFREDO: It's a respectable corporation and you don't know anything! Get out of here!

RENÉ: Right. I don't have proof of anything. (*Takes a step toward him. Frightened, ALFREDO threatens him with a punch, but RENÉ evades it and covers his mouth with one hand, throwing him at the same time into one of the side chairs where he forces him to sit and not cry out.*) I'd like to squash you like a scorpion, but I won't. Your servants would be all over me in a moment and that thug in the hallway would dispatch me without giving it a second thought. And even if we were alone, I still wouldn't do it. So don't call for help. (*HE releases him and steps away.*) I'm dead too since Sandra died. But I'll live on for a fight that's necessary. That's how I'll fight against you, not here with my fists.

ALFREDO (*HE has listened to René with increasing despair and finally hides his face in his hands*): I no longer want to live.

RENÉ (*Moves toward him aggressively, but controls himself*): Hypocrite. You haven't put an end to your life in all these days, and you won't. You want to go on living... I prefer that. That way you'll suffer a few more years.

ALFREDO: Why fight, here or there? You haven't wanted to understand me... I'm sorry about our fight; I shouldn't have provoked it. (*Uncovers his face and looks at him.*) Stay and head my foundation. We'll remember Sandra... together.

RENÉ (*Sardonically*): Still trying? (*HE goes closer and lowers his voice.*) I'm weak too. I confess that was my greatest temptation: to stay here comfortably and be with Sandra always. But you can't tempt me any more. Go on alone in front of your video, play it a thousand times. You won't see anything but your own horror.

ALFREDO (*Almost begging*): That unites us too...

RENÉ: No. Look at yourself on that screen. Frozen at age twenty. (*Ironically*) Time in your hands? Don't deceive yourself; you, sir, in the hands of time. (*HE turns Alfredo's face forcibly toward the video screen.*) Look! Back then you didn't know what you were going to make of your own daughter; if you run it to the end, you'll see that she's dead. It's the only answer you'll get from all the faces of your life: death.

ALFREDO (*HE gets up very shaken*): She was a crazy girl determined not to take precautions! I didn't kill her!

RENÉ: No? What do you think that other crazy person was who murdered her?

ALFREDO: I don't know!

RENÉ: Yes you do. A drug addict. The danger you never wanted to name. And you were on the point of his knife. (*With black arm band and tie, JAVIER has reached the telephone in the corner at left and begun to dial under the cold light of a spot.*)

ALFREDO: No! (*Exasperated, HE goes toward the window.*)

RENÉ (*Pronouncing implacably*):   Mundifisa. (*The telephone rings. ALFREDO looks at RENÉ with indecision.*)

ALFREDO (*Picks up receiver*): Hello.

JAVIER: Papa, there's news. They've arrested the murderer and he's confessed.

ALFREDO: Who is he?

JAVIER: The name's not important. A seventeen year old boy. Out of his mind at that moment, of course. And high on cocaine. (*Silence.*) Did you hear what I said?

ALFREDO (*His voice failing him.*): Yes.

JAVIER: He'll get what he deserves, don't worry. (*Another silence.*) Are you listening to me? What's wrong with you?

ALFREDO: Nothing.

JAVIER: Papa, cheer up. We have to be strong when fate deals us a blow.

ALFREDO: Fate?

JAVIER: Of course. And we'll learn to guard ourselves even better from chance happenings. I'll come see you this afternoon. We'll talk. We'll go for a walk.

ALFREDO (*In an outburst*): Withdraw all our money from that abomination immediately! (*HE immediately regrets what he has said and looks at RENÉ out of the corner of his eye. RENÉ observes him with a disdainful sneer.*)

JAVIER: Are you out of your mind? It's impossible at this moment.

ALFREDO (*Moderating his tone*): Do it.

JAVIER: It's impossible! We'll talk about it later. (*HE hangs up and exits. The corner is dark again. Wrapped in his thoughts, ALFREDO puts down the phone.*)

RENÉ: In effect, it's impossible.

ALFREDO: What?

RENÉ: Do you think I couldn't figure out what you were talking about? (*A slight gesture toward the VCR.*) Maybe before, when you were young, you could choose. Now you can't. But I can! And I'm going. With empty hands. I'm returning to my country, where we're trying to keep the rich from getting richer and the poor poorer.

ALFREDO (*Somberly*): Your country is already corrupted.

RENÉ: It may be. But there the corruption is born from misery, not from wealth. (*HE crosses and stops before He goes out the door.*) Don't make another video of Sandra like that one. It would be useless, just like yours is. (*Holding back the tears.*) It won't bring her back to life... And you won't live again either. You can't play around with time. (*Exits. With unsure steps, ALFREDO goes toward the side chairs, takes the remote control and sits before the video screen, turning the tape on frantically. The livid glow from the monitor screen falls on the disturbed face of the financier. Cold shadows fall over the room. It seems to ALFREDO that he hears the ghostly voice of his daughter, and he stops the tape without turning off the set.)*

SANDRA *(Her icy voice):* Good-bye, my father. I'm going too. With him and forever... I'll join him... in our eternal afternoon. Good-bye... Good-bye... Good-bye... *(When silence returns, ALFREDO fixes his staring eyes on the video. The adagio from Mozart's First Concerto for flute and orchestra reaches from the courtyard like a musical caress. The morning light brings a mood of serenity again. ALFREDO looks up and listens. Suddenly he drops the remote control on the chair beside him and gets up, his thoughts on the window. The facing window is opening. With yearning, ALFREDO rushes to his. A woman with some sewing in her hand has just opened the shutters. She wears glasses and looking up toward the sky, breathes happily the first air of summer. As SHE sits down by the window, she notices that ALFREDO is watching her. It is the same woman who appeared earlier in memory, but her appearance has changed noticeably. SHE is prematurely aged, and there are circles under her eyes from fatigue. There are deep lines around her mouth and her hair, carelessly arranged, is almost white. Both surprised and annoyed, SHE takes off her glasses and looks frowning at ALFREDO for several long moments.)*

ALFREDO *(Holding on to the window frame, HE is hardly audible):* Isolina... *(With a brusque movement and loud slam, the woman closes her window. ALFREDO turns around with downcast eyes and walks over to a chair into which HE collapses. The music goes on. The light fades. In the invading darkness, only the faded woman's closed window still stands out under the morning sunlight.)*

CURTAIN

CRITICAL REACTION IN SPAIN

"As is customary in his dramatic mode, Buero situates the action on various temporal planes. There are successive yesterdays that will be revealed and which will unveil the truth about the characters in the ever valid manner of Ibsen; and he grafts onto the temporal reality of that richly furnished sitting room his constant paraverbal elements: ... classical music that refers to other moments and other emotions, the impossible window that opens like a beckoning call from the past... behind which music incites to an impossible recovery from the past... *Música cercana* (*The Music Window*) remains true to Buero's enduring concerns, both social and political."

> Lorenzo López Sancho
> *ABC* (Madrid)
> 23 September 1989

"*Música cercana* (*The Music Window*) is, in terms of plot, a tremendous parable about the price ambition can pay. In its details, it is a story about today, whose immediate references can be found in any weekly publication that reports on the world of big business and the people who control it. It may also seem a fable about good and bad, about people who are archangelic or demoniacal...."

> Carlos Bacigalupe
> *El correo español-El pueblo vasco*
> 20 August 1989

64

ABOUT THE TRANSLATOR

Marion Peter Holt is a member of the doctoral faculty in theatre at the Graduate Center of the City University of New York and professor of Spanish Literature and Translation at CUNY's College of Staten Island. He has also taught "Translation for the Stage" in the Interdisciplinary Program in Translation at the Graduate Center. In 1985, *Choice*, named his collection *Antonio Buero-Vallejo: Three Plays* an outstanding university press book of the year. His translations of Spanish and Latin American plays have been staged in New York and London, in Australia, and by regional and university theatres throughout the United States. In 1986 he was elected a corresponding member of the Real Academia Española.

TRANSLATOR'S NOTE AND ACKNOWLEDGEMENTS

This English version of *Música cercana* restores all the cuts made in the script of the original Madrid production of 1989. These amount to an occasional line or phrase and a section of some 15 lines near the end of Part I. Any variations from the order of the dialogue or absence of a phrase result from the normal process of recreating a script in a new language. As noted on the cast page, the bits of dialogue originally spoken by Lorenza in English are now in Spanish, with the original English retained in brackets. A director may prefer to find a different solution by changing the expressions to French or some other language, or by simply having them spoken in English as asides. In any case, Lorenza's caustic interjections are essential to her character and to an authentic performance of Buero's play.

I wish to express my appreciation to Martha T. Halsey for the ongoing efforts that make the *Estreno* Play Translations possible, to Phyllis Zatlin for invaluable advice, and to the Dirección General del Libro y Bibliotecas of the Spanish Ministery of Culture for the financial assistance that made this English version possible. I am particularly grateful to Phil Alexander and Andrew Erdman of the Ph.D. program in Theatre of the City University of New York for their skillful assistance in preparing the computer copy for this edition.

M.P.H.

ESTRENO: CONTEMPORARY SPANISH PLAYS SERIES
General Editor: Martha T. Halsey

No. 1   Jaime Salom: *Bonfire at Dawn*
        Translated by Phyllis Zatlin. 1992.
No. 2   José López Rubio: *In August We Play the Pyrenees*
        Translated by Marion P. Holt. 1992.
No. 3   Ramón del Valle-Inclán: *Savage Acts: Four Plays*
        Translated by Robert Lima. 1993.
No. 4   Antonio Gala: *The Bells of Orleans*
        Translated by Edward Borsoi. 1993.
No. 5   Antonio Buero-Vallejo: *The Music Window*
        Translated by Marion P. Holt. 1994.
No. 6   Paloma Pedrero: *Parting Gestures: Three by Pedrero*
        Translated by Phyllis Zatlin. 1994.
No. 7   Ana Diosdado: *Yours for the Asking*
        Translated by Patricia W. O'Connor. 1995.

- -

ORDER FORM
Quantity   Title

_____   _____

_____   _____

_____   _____

Please include payment at $6.00 per copy, postpaid.

Name and address: _____

                  _____

                  _____

Mail to: ESTRENO   Telephone: 814/865-1122
          350 N. Burrowes Bldg.   FAX: 814/863-7944
          University Park, PA 16802 USA